Walk with Me

Danielle Walker

DEDICATION

To GOD and GOD alone.

CONTENTS

ACKNOWLEDGMENTS

First, I would like to give honor to my Lord and Savior Jesus Christ and send a huge shout out to Him for the blood He shed on Calvary for me to have a right to the 'Tree of Life' and an opportunity to be considered a Kingdom Kid. I want to give reverence to GOD my BOO creator of all things the one and only 'I AM'. I can't do nothing without you and I am nothing without you. I want to thank you for considering me when you created your plan to populate Earth. I don't take this opportunity for granted because I know that I could have been upon the many that didn't make it into this life or one of the many that didn't have the opportunity to share your breath that you placed within me. And I thank you from the bottom of my heart for counting me worthy enough to be placed on this Earth to serve you and to love you and to share your message with your people. I count it all joy the day you spoke my name and will forever strive to please you in all of my ways. Thank you and I will love you always, Dannie.

UNDERSTANDING

I would like to start by saying I have no idea of how this book is going to turn out. All I ask is that you flow with me and just keep reading. Be open to what you may find and I pray that whatever is shared is something that you will be able to hold on to when you find yourself in a time of need or even in a rejoiceful place. No I'm not a subject matter expert and to be honest the way this book came about, I was sitting at my desk at work and a burst of inspiration came while I was attempting to start preparing for bible study. Isn't that ironic. Funny because I've struggled with writer's block for almost a year now and I still haven't finished the other book I'm supposed to be working on.

I want to take this time to go ahead and answer the question, before you begin to ask it yourself. This book is going to be a body of work that I have studied and received revelation from the information that I've read. You will find this book as a source to help you understand some of the stories that I've read in the bible through my own experience and understanding of it. Again, I am not an expert and never will I profess to be. I am only a student and a willing vessel to share what I have experienced in hopes that it encourages you on your journey as it did me. Before we begin I want to encourage you to grab a pencil and a notepad for it will be a blessing unto you to jot down any key information you find to circle back on your down time to study. Yes, I will be writing down information as well because this is going to be a learning opportunity for me also. I say this because this is truly going to be my first book that I compile off the top of my head as it comes to me. So, nervous. But, I trust GOD.

How many mistakes will you make before you give up the ghost? (Three strikes and you're out)

Question: What crossed your mind after reading our first topic? Did it make you nervous? Did it prompt you to think about everything you've done in your past that you or society may constitute as being wrong? Did you read over it as if you're reading the title of a new chapter? Or, have you took no thought into it at all?

On September 14, 2014, I had the pleasure of ministering my first sermon ever. My dad announced in front of the church congregation the Sunday prior that I would be bringing the word that coming Sunday and I was petrified. I've never preached a day in my life. Plus, I'd just flunked out of public speaking due to my fear of 'Public Speaking'. The sweat started pouring immediately and by the end of the benediction my armpit patch was wet as ever. The fear was real. It's like I can feel the anxiety all over again.

I would love to say that after four years the anxiety has subsided and I'm more relaxed and confident in myself when I stand behind the pulpit. But, my story didn't play out that way. I think I may be even more nervous now than I was back then. The reasonings may have changed, due to the stares no longer scare me. Now, the fear is in hoping no one is misled by my own personal accounts of what took place from what I read. And that the messages I believe the Lord shares with me to share with His people is relayed in the way that He wants it to be relayed. The weight is heavy and I don't take it likely, because that's a lot of blood on your hands every time you stand in front of a crowd.

With this new responsibility and with no real experience. I inquired of the Lord what would He like for me to speak about to His people. And on September 9, 2014, He responded and gave me the title listed above. Excited that I got an immediate answer. I burst out into one of the biggest cool aids I could muster up. I had no idea of what to do with the title, all I knew is I was excited. I think the saddest part about the whole situation was the fact that I didn't know where the message would come from within the word to help me make the topic make sense. (Trust I'm laughing out loud right here).

What I've learned thus far is that when GOD has something for you, it's truly meant for you. You can stress out about it all you want. You can even try and run from it, but you will yield. Whether its willingly or involuntarily. You decide. So let's start by defining a few key terms.

Terms

- Humble- Having or showing a modest or low estimate of one's own importance.
- Mistake- an action or judgement that is misguided or wrong.
- Strike- cancel, remove, or cross out with or as if with a pen.
- Death- the action or fact of dying or being killed; the end of the life of a person or organism.   {-Webster}

Whenever my dad calls on me to give a sermon. I like to research key terms that are relevant to what we will be leaning. I'm not sure if anyone else does this, but it helps me personally when it comes to breaking down what certain statements mean and also helps me understand how the terms relate. In this section we will be learning and reviewing for some the story of Daniel, Nebuchadnezzar, and Belshazzar. The way the studies are going to be outlined will be as follows: I'll give the title, key terms with definition, the verses, a breakdown of what I understood from it, and then close out each with supporting random verses to support the message. Are you ready? Let's dive in.

Daniel 5:21-22

'And he was driven from the sons of men; and his heart was made like the beasts, and his dwelling was with the wild asses: they fed him with grass like oxen, and his body was wet with the dew of heaven; till he knew that the most high God ruled in the kingdom of men, and that he appointeth over it whomsoever he will. And thou his son, O Belshazzar, hast not humbled thine heart, though thou knewest all this;' -KJV

Here in these two verses we see Daniel is reminding Belshazzar. Even though, you know what happened to your father. You still have chosen to do wrong against God. And now He has a message for you that He has written personally.

Daniel 5:25-31

'And this is the writing that was written, MENE, MENE, TEKEL, UPHARSIN. This is the interpretation of the thing: MENE; God hath numbered thy kingdom, and finished it. TEKEL; Thou art weighed in the balances, and art found wanting. PERES; Thy kingdom is divided, and given to the Medes and Persians. Then commanded Belshazzar, and they clothed Daniel with scarlet, and put a chain of gold about his neck, and made a proclamation concerning him, that he should be the third ruler in the kingdom. In that night was Belshazzar the king of the Chaldeans slain. And Darius the median took the kingdom, being about threescore and two years old.' -

KJV

Belshazzar wasn't given a second chance to make a mistake. He was punished instantly. What I got from this story which caused me to assume that the Lord shed no mercy on Belshazzar is because his father mistakes that he repeatedly made was the warning. A warning that Belshazzar was fully aware of and he still chose to disobey thinking he might get the same leniency. How many of us can admit to doing things we knew were wrong and yet we did them anyway, because we felt if we repented all would be forgiven. I can. But, what if God treated us as He did Belshazzar. Would that not be a frightening thing to experience. Aren't you glad that we serve a merciful God. I know I am.

Daniel 5:20

'But when his heart was lifted up, and his mind hardened in pride, he was deposed from his kingly throne, and they took his glory from him:' -KJV

God has a way of showing us who's in control. Take Nebuchadnezzar as an example. When Nebuchadnezzar made his gods, he was full of pride. Are any of us still battling with pride ourselves. He wanted to force the people to worship his images that he presented, but GOD said not so. He used three of His faithful servants as a witness to the power He possess and no man or beast or image can do or have. Later we find that Nebuchadnezzar accepted 'GOD' but he still chose not to serve Him, until everything was taken away. But why wait until you're cast out of your kingdom to profess "GOD" is the one and only "True and Living God".

Have you found yourself in a place to where you have placed someone else in Gods spot? He can never be replaced. Recognize if you haven't already, that we do serve a jealous God. With that being said, it's only so

5

long and so far He'd let you go with the disrespect. Now you may get away with some things when you are ignorant to the truth. However, once you become knowledgeable to what's real, then judgement has begun.

It amazes me how throughout the entire book of Daniel. In the beginning these kings are trying to create 'gods' to worship through images made of gold. Instead of worshiping the 'GOD' that sits high and looks low. Again, my Father is a jealous God. And who are we to give his glory to someone or something else. Let's take a moment for self-reflection. Are there any 'gods' in your life that are blocking you from serving the one who created all things? If so, let's do what's necessary to start moving towards making a change. We start simply by renouncing the old beliefs and accepting the new and then asking for forgiveness and understanding. I truly believe in doing that GOD hears and accepts all repentance of heart with the confession of the tongue mercifully. Doesn't it feel good to serve Elohim.

REVIVAL

Now that we've established the atmosphere of where we will be operating in moving forward. How do you feel about our time together so far? Are you excited to learn more about Gods word? Have you noticed any changes in your mood so far? Do you feel like you can hold on just a little while longer? I do. I can't remember the first day that I was introduced to the Lord, but I do remember that I've always had a relationship with Him. When I think back on my childhood coming up in A New Apostolic Holiness Deliverance Church. I can remember all of the long hours, sleepovers that were called 'Shut In's', the Choir competitions that weren't really competitions. I say this because we were actually just visiting our fellow sister churches and it was custom that all the choirs sing and we would get up there and act like no one could sing better than us nine.

Have you ever experienced a revival? I mean a real Holy Ghost filled revival. Not one of those gatherings some churches put together for show and they call them a revival, that's where you would refer to it as attending. Well if you haven't, let me bring you up to speed of what takes place. On the first night which is usually a Friday, you come as you are. Most people are just leaving work so there's really no time to go home and change, because it normally starts at 7:00 p.m.. When you get there most people are tired and a little sleepy because it's been a hectic week and they're usually coming only to be supportive of someone or because the Pastor made it mandatory to attend.

Depending on how big the church is the first person that greets you is going to be the greeter standing at the door to welcome you. If it's a smaller church, then you'll be greeted by the usher and that individual is either going to allow you to choose your own seating if you've arrived early enough or lead you down to your seat next to someone who've you've possibly never met before. But trust me, by the end of the night. You've just made a brand new friend. Usually by this time once the people have all started migrating to the sanctuary, this prompts the initiation of intercessory prayer. This special prayer is where we welcome the Lord into the room and ask Him to bless the service and have free reign. Then services begins with devotion and everything that follows.

Now, when it comes to the devotion services. It can go either way for me. When it's done right, the whole congregation is in a frenzy and there's no doubt in your mind that the Lord has entered into the room. And at that point I'm just beside myself with praise. Done wrong, it kind of feels like maybe the Lord has done a drive-by and kept going because you can sense that the worship isn't for real. When in those type of situations, you can tell I'm ready to go. And my patience is slim to none. Because I enjoy hearing the word, my favorite part of the service is always going to be the time when the minister is called to give the message for the evening. That's where I come alive. Have you ever heard of a hype man? If so, consider me the hype woman. I tend to be one of the loudest people in the room, but I digress. This is where the meat of the meal is placed on the plate and if by chance you were one of the individuals that came in down or unmoved. This is the moment of rejuvenation. I can't tell you what happens between the time you get out of your car up until this point of hearing the sermon.

All I can assure you is you'll be excited beyond recognition. The love, the joy, the warmth, acceptance, and the sense of belonging you feel is like nothing you've ever experienced outside of a Holy Ghost filled service. After the benediction, you feel like new money anticipating the Saturday's service. Which leads us over into our next topic.

A Fathers Love
"Sinners saved by grace"

Question: Have you ever been in love? Or, have you ever desired the love from someone else? Have you ever pondered on the love that your parents have for you? Have you ever considered the love that you have for your parents? It's something unconditional right. I've found through experience that we never really think about the love we share with our parents, it's just automatic. If something happens to them in a negative or positive way, it affects us emotionally instantly once we're made aware of it. What about the love between us and our Heavenly Father. Do you think He's moved emotionally when things happen to us. If not, then why not. I believe He is. I say this because how can someone create a being with feels and He not know what's it's like to feel those same emotions. Let's go a little deeper with a few terms.

Terms
- Love- an intense feeling of deep affection.
- Father- a man in relation to his natural child or children. A man who gives care and protection to someone or something. (in Christian belief) the first person of the Trinity; God
- Sinner- a person who transgresses against divine law by committing

an immortal act or acts.

- Saved- keep safe or rescue (someone or something) from harm or danger. (in Christian use) preserve (a person's soul) from damnation.

- Grace- (in Christian belief) the free and unmerited favor of God, as manifested in the salvation of sinners and the bestowal of blessings. {Webster}

There's nothing like the love of a father. Growing up I didn't have my dad in the house with me but I did go and spend the night from time to time. And on some occasions he would come and pick me up just to take me to work with him. He could do no wrong in my eyes and even when he did. I always had room in my heart to forgive him every single time.

Luke 15: 18-24

'I will arise and go to my father, and will say unto him, Father, I have sinned against heaven, and before thee, And am no more worthy to be called thy son: make me as one of thy hired servants. And he arose, and came to his father. But when he was yet a great way off, his father saw him, and had compassion, and ran, and fell on his neck, and kissed him. And the son said unto him, Father, I have sinned against heaven, and in thy sight, and am no more worthy to be called son. But the father said to his servants, Bring forth the best robe, and put it on him; and put a ring on his hand, and shoes on his feet: And bring hither the fatted calf, and kill it; and let us eat, and be merry: For this my son was dead, and is alive again; he was lost, and is found. And they began to be merry.' -KJV

Here in this text we have an awesome example of unconditional love between a father and his son. Let's break down what transpired up to this point. There once was a man who had two sons and one day the youngest of the two went to his father and asked for his inheritance. He didn't want to wait until his dad died to get what was promised to him. He wanted it in his present state while he was still young I'm assuming to enjoy it. Well, the dad didn't argue the request and made the decision to give both his sons their inheritance at the same time. Let's pause right here for a quick discussion.

If someone was to walk up to you right now and give you a million dollars, what would you do. Would you be responsible and pay all of your debts down to zero and sit on the remaining money or would you go out and ball for a short period of time. Seriously, I want you to take five seconds to consider what you would do. Now, after those five take another minute to consider what you would do if you were still a teenager or in your early twenties and just got loaded with all this cash. Speaking for Danielle, I know at this point of my life if I came across a million dollars and it was mine to keep. I would pay off all of my debt and sit on the rest for a year and not say nothing to no one about it. I can say this because I've already had this discussion with myself when I attempted to play the mega millions.

However, if it was the younger Danielle. That money would've been blown in so many different ways I can't even begin to count. Yes, I'm sure I would've gotten myself out of debt. But, I can assure you I would've went and created even more debt than I had to begin with, because I've been debt free twice in my life and here I am with more debt again. Maturity stems from experience. Experience comes through the process of trial and error. How would you know not to touch the iron because it's hot when it's plugged up. If you've never felt the heat.

Let's pick up where we left off. If you read the entire chapter 15 in the book of Luke in which I strongly encourage you to do. You will find in the text that the younger son that inquired of his father for his portion, is the one who went out and blew it. The story teller never made mention of the fellows age. He only acknowledges the fact that he was the youngest of the two. And after falling on hard times, he found himself in a place of shame.

Have you ever done something so shameful that you would rather wallow in your own pity party, instead of reaching out for help. Well, that's exactly what this young man had done. He was so prideful in the beginning that he found himself amongst the pigs and eventually he made a conscious decision to go back to his father to be taken back in. This time as a servant.

Back when I was nineteen, my mom kicked me out of the house. The ideal thing for me to say is that I did nothing to deserve it, but I did. The first night I was out I was so full of anger that I called everyone I knew to see if I could come and stay with them due to my now circumstance and what I found were unexpected fees and a few no's. After playing the last card I had to play by calling my grandma. She told me to go back home because it was her house and not my mom's. When I went back me and my mom didn't speak for a few days if I can remember correctly, and then I broke. I apologized and then she opened up and explained to me why she did what she'd done.

Walking into his father's house. I know the guy didn't anticipate his dad to be happy that he came home and ready to celebrate his return. Have you ever been shocked by someone's excitement to see you when you expected grief. Time heals all wombs. However, the text never mentioned the father ever being angry with his son for asking for his inheritance.

Luke 15: 27-32

'And he said unto him, Thy brother is come; and thy father hath killed the fatted calf,

because he hath received him safe and sound. And he was angry, and would not go in: therefore came his father out, and intreated him. And he answering said to his father, Lo, these many years do I serve thee, neither transgressed I at any time thy commandment: and yet thou never gavest me a kid, that I might make merry with my friends: But as soon as this thy son was come, which hath devoured thy living with harlots, thou hast killed for him the fatted calf. And he said unto him, Son, thou art ever with me, and all that I have is thine. It was meet that we should make merry, and be glad: for this thy brother was dead, and is alive again; and was lost, and is found.' -KJV

As you can see after the return of the younger son the eldest became jealous. He couldn't understand how his father could celebrate his return after he'd made a mockery of himself out in the streets and spent all of his money. And yet, his father still welcomed him back with open and loving arms. What I saw was a father happy that his son was alive and not dead. We can only assume the torment the father went through mentally and emotionally, everyday his son was gone. Telephones weren't around in these times. Therefore he had no way of knowing if he was dead or alive. So, he assumed the worst. Have you ever got out of contact with someone dear to you and the last time you spoke with them weren't on the best terms. Have you ever wondered what happened to them. Or, do you treat them as though you've never crossed paths.

Is there someone out there that you need to forgive for doing you wrong. Or, is there someone that you may need to seek out and ask for forgiveness for how you treated them. Know that it is ok to make mistakes, but you have to learn from them. Make amends where mending is needed. And if someone happens to come back into your life seeking forgiveness, don't do like the elder brother and harden your heart. Be an example like the father and extend that mercy to that individual. You never know what they've endured in that time apart. Your forgiveness could be the thing that can lift the heaviness from their heart as well. Be kind and know you're not always the one standing on the right side of wrong.

I want to leave you with a few verses/nuggets to help you during this season of your life. Remember them, write them on the table of your heart, and know that you always have a guide to help you through any situation.

Matthew 4:17

'From that time Jesus began to preach, and to say, Repent: for the kingdom of heaven is at hand.' -KJV

It's important that we take the time if we haven't already and ask God to forgive us for everything that we've ever done that wasn't pleasing in His eyesight. Why is this important you ask? Because we can't make it into heaven without a repentant heart. Also, when you take the time to ask the Lord to forgive you, be sure you're really ready to be forgiven. Don't do it just because someone suggested it to you. Do it because YOU want to and you're ready. This walk is between you and Him and only He has the last and final say.

Mark 12:29-31

'And Jesus answered him, The first of all commandments is, Hear, O Israel; The Lord our God is one Lord. And thou shalt love the Lord thy God with all thy heart, and with all thy soul, and with all thy mind, and with all thy strength: this is the first commandment. And the second is like, namely this, Thou shalt love thy neighbor as thyself. There is none other commandment greater than these.' -KJV

If you take nothing else away from this passage, take this. Love God no matter what and love people even if they've wronged you. You can love them and not be around them, but you have to love them.

John 3:16

'For God so loved the world, that he gave his only begotten Son, that whosoever believeth in him should not perish, but have everlasting life.' -KJV

What greater love? If you've had the opportunity to be blessed enough to have children, think about it. Are you willing to allow someone to kill your child willingly to save someone that disrespects you and treat you like you don't matter? Or, treat you like you don't exist and your sacrifice meant nothing? How would that make you feel? Have you ever thought about it? Can you imagine the grief? Not just the grief of the death, but the grief of how people are treating you after the fact when you've done this thing for their benefit. I haven't been blessed to bare children yet, but I already am in a place where I have a strong heck to the no lock and prepared to shout. Think back when God asked Abraham to sacrifice Issac. God will never ask of us something He wouldn't do himself. Oh, what love.

Romans 10:9

'That if thou shalt confess with thy mouth the Lord Jesus, and shalt believe in thine heart that God hath raised him from the dead, thou shalt be saved.' -KJV

It's one thing to believe something, but you have to say it. Here's your chance to make a declaration that can and will save your life. I am a strong believer that we as people are afraid to do things in a public atmosphere where we are subjected to others opinion. Well baby, let me be the first to tell you. You are alone with your thoughts and plenty of opportunity. What are you going to do?

Revelation 3:20

'Behold, I stand at the door, and knock: if any man hear my voice, and open the door, I will come in to him, and will sup with him, and he with me.' -KJV

What I took from this message was that God attempts to reach us and if we open our hearts to receive His nudge and acknowledge that He is speaking. Then, He will chat with us as much as we like.

Ephesians 6:11

'Put on the whole armour of God, that ye may be able to stand against the wiles of the devil.' -KJV

Luke 21:36

'Watch ye therefore, and pray always, that ye may be accounted worthy to escape all these things that shall come to pass, and to stand before the Son of man.' KJV

Be vigilant.

Revelation 22:7

'Behold, I come quickly: blessed is he that keepeth the sayings of the prophecy of this book.' -KJV

Revelation 16:15

'Behold, I come as a thief. Blessed is he that watcheth, and keepeth his garments, lest he walk naked, and they see his shame.' -KJV

Always be aware of the times and how the changes that are taking place in our world today align with the word of God. I know for some this may be the only thing that you'll ever have that can give you a glimpse of what was written in times past. That's why I'm taking my time to place certain scriptures in this book to help you along in your faith walk. There will come a time when the bible will no longer be accessible to the believers and if you don't have it memorized there would be a great loss. But aren't you glad that God saw fit to give us all another way to access what's important and what He would have us all to know. Who wouldn't want to serve a God like ours?

Are you still with me? If you've made it to this sentence baby pat yourself on the back, because you are a trooper. I'm excited that you've made it this far. I'm thrilled that you've not only took time aside to mature in your faith, but your intrigue to want to learn more excites me alone. If no one has ever told you that they're proud of you. I want to take this opportunity to tell you Danielle Walker is very proud of you and I know our Lord is smiling down on you sunshine.

I want you to take a moment to review what you've learned so far. Don't try and read everything in one sitting. Take a moment and let everything sit in and try some of the actions that were listed about in the text. Forgive those who've wronged you and ask for forgiveness from those you've wronged. Open up an opportunity for the Lord to speak to you. How? Sit in silence and start to pray and ask Him to speak. Usually, once you stop making requests He'll speak. How? Threw the thoughts you get. Did you know that? It tripped me out too when I first figured it out. I was waiting to hear some loud voice come out of nowhere. But, being as scary as I am with certain things. I was like 'Lord please don't let it be some random voice out loud that's going to scare me', and then later I figured He speaks to us in our thoughts. You'll learn the difference in time.

You ready for our next topic. I am, lets dive right in. Also, don't be afraid to share this book with a friend or a relative. You never know what people are going through and how you sharing this with them can bless them and turn their situation around.

PROMISES

Have you ever made a promise before? Have you ever reneged on that promise? Did you know every time you tell someone you are going to do something you are making them a promise. I know right, shocking. Do you know some of the promises that God have made to you since birth? I encourage you to research them. I can assure you He is the ONLY one who never reneges on His promises. His word is sure. We may experience a delay due to some of the choices we make, or even our own laziness to go and get them. But, they are yes and amen.

Trust Fund
"Delayed not Denied"

In my adolescent years I would spend my weekends either at my dad's, nana's, friend's, aunt's, or great grandmothers house. When it came time for me to spend time with my dad, he would call and tell me when I needed to be ready for him to come and pick me up. Enthused with excitement, I would rush home after school on those Fridays and load my bags down. You couldn't tell me nothing. I was a daddy's girl and no matter what happened I would always remain a daddy's girl. However, you would think time after time that he stood me up waiting in the we-hours of the morning looking for him to come. I would've learned my lesson and stopped getting my hopes up when he told me he was coming. But, I never learned. My mom would try and convince me to stop getting my hopes up knowing he would sometimes break his promise and come the next day. But, forgiving as I was and being a daddy's girl. When he told me he was going to do something I held on to it for dear life. Do you know still to this day if my dad called me and said he was going to do something I would get that same excitement and believe him even if he fails me. I still give him that chance to be a man of his word.

Terms

- Trust fund- is a fund comprised of a variety of assets intended to provide benefits to an individual or organization. The trust fund is established by a grantor to provide financial security to an individual, most often a child or grandchild.
- Delay- postponed or defer; to put off to a later time.
- Denied- (deny)- refuse to give or grant (something requested or desired) to (someone).   {-Webster}

Malachi 3:8-12

Will a man rob God? Yet ye have robbed me. But ye say, Wherein have we robbed thee? In tithes and offerings. Ye are cursed with a curse: for ye have robbed me, even this whole nation. Bring ye all the tithes into the storehouse, that there may be meat in mine house, and prove me now herewith, saith the Lord of hosts, if I will not open you the windows of heaven, and pour you out a blessing, that there shall not be room enough to receive it. And I will rebuke the devourer for your sakes, and he shall not destroy the fruits of your ground; neither shall your vine cast her fruit before the time in the field, saith the Lord of hosts. And all nations shall call you blessed: for ye shall be a delightsome land, saith the Lord of hosts.' -KJV

Money has always been a sensitive topic, especially in the African American community. No one ever wants to talk about it and when they do everyone cringe, try bringing it up in church. You can hear the crickets chirping from the outside anytime the subject is mentioned. You have to begin to ask yourself what has happened to cause the congregation to no longer desire to give freely to the church. Yes, some can say due to the miss use of the money. Others lean towards not wanting to support monetarily for their own personal reasons, and the remaining that do give. Don't give the tenth that God has charged us to give. Why?

Before I came into the understanding of what tithing was, my mom and grandparents already had me trained to do so. As I got older and came into the knowledge of what it meant to give the Lord back what He gave me. The money couldn't get in my hand quick enough before I've already calculated what I was placing in the offering. I don't say this to brag. I want to you understand what you are doing to yourself voluntarily.

When you give God your tenth, you are not only showing gratitude and appreciation for the portion He has blessed you with. But, you are securing any future endeavor you may want to partake in. Have you ever heard the saying 'you reap what you sow'. Consider this, if a farmer never plant his seeds in the planting season. He can't expect food when it's time for the fruits and vegetables to give off their harvest. You can't expect God to bless you in your finances if you've never blessed Him through your finances. You are cursing yourself in that area. So what if you think the pastor is using the money in a dishonest way. That's none of your concern, you've done your part. God will bless you and deal with that pastor.

Don't allow someone else's bad experiences hinder you from benefiting from what the kingdom has to offer. It's almost like the commandment we learnt earlier to love our neighbor. If we have to love them in spit of, then you have to give in the same context. Sometimes the one thing you've been praying and asking God for is being held up because you're not willing to do the one thing he asks of you. How can He trust you with a million dollars when you wont use it to bless a church that may actually be doing good work in the community for the less fortunate. Consider the homeless person that you passed at that red light. Have you ever gave to one of those individuals? What if the shoe was on the other foot. Have you ever considered that it could be you. But, God.

Deuteronomy 14:22

'Thou shalt truly tithe all the increase of thy seed, that the field bringeth forth year by year.' -KJV

If the IRS can get their tenth before you even see your check. Why can't you voluntarily bless God after you've received? The difference between the two. You can't depend on one to stretch the remaining so you can have enough to cover all of your obligations and get some things you want because you desire them. But you can always be rest assured the other will always make a way out of no way for you.

2 Corinthians 9:7-11

'Every man according as he purpospeth in his heart, so let him give; not grudgingly, or of necessity: for God loveth a cheerful giver. And God is able to make all grace abound toward you; that ye, always having all sufficiency in all things, may abound to every good work: (As it is written, He hath dispersed abroad; he hath given to the poor: his righteousness remaineth for ever. Now he that ministereth seed to the sower both minister

bread for your food, and multiply your seed sown, and increase the fruits of your righteousness;) Being enriched in every thing to all bountifulness, which causeth through us thanksgiving to God.' -KJV

2 Corinthians 9:6

'But this I say, He which soweth sparingly shall reap also sparingly; and he which soweth bountifully shall reap also bountifully.' -KJV

How powerful is that statement. To my understanding it means if you give a dollar then you get what a dollars blessing is worth. Now if it's your last dollar and you give it then that holds a heavier weight because it was all you had and you gave it anyway. Oh, what a sacrifice.

Luke 6:38

'Give, and it shall be given unto you; good measure, pressed down, and shaken together, and running over, shall men give into your bosom. For with the same measure that ye mete withal it shall be measured to you again.' -KJV

God's word will never return to him void. You can rest assure, if He said it was going to come to pass. It's going to happen. He is not lie man. He spoke light and there was light. And God said, let there be a firmament in the mist of the waters and it came forth. And God said, Let the waters under the heaven be gathered together unto one place, and let the dry land appear; and it was so. And God said, Let the earth bring forth grass, the herb yielding seed, and the fruit tree yielding fruit after his kind and it was so. Everything that God say comes to fruition that's why every promise again is yes and amen.

I charge you from this moment forward to live by the word you give.

If you say you are going to do something, do it. Even if you foresee that you won't be able to keep your word. Share that with the person and arrange to do it at a later time. You got this champ. I believe in you.

AWARENESS

Are you afraid of the dark. I know you're thinking who starts a sentence off with 'are you afraid of the dark'. I do. I've never really figured out if I am or not, but what I do know is I still sleep with the hall light on. Yes, I freak out when it's off. I freak out when the entire house is pitch black and no one else is in the house with me. Even if they are, I'm racing to get next to them. I've concluded I do this because I wear glasses. Having the ability to see my surroundings is very important to me. For those of you who have 20/20 vision I hope you never learn the struggle of forgetting where you've laid your eyes. What if there's a big o 'l spider on the wall or an ancient rat lurking in the corner of your kitchen cabinets. What will you do? Who's going to warn you of those dangers when the lights go out?

How aware of your surroundings are you. When we enter into the institution of kindergarten, we begin to learn about our senses. Our sense of touch, taste, smell, hearing, and vision. I learned fairly early you can still thrive without a few of them. I have a aunt by the name of Charlene and she's blind. She wasn't born blind, but she became blind at an adolescent age. If you were to ever meet aunt Charlene you'd never believe she didn't have sight. She cooks, cleans, does hair, write letters, shop, ride the Marta bus, everything you can do she can do. I remember me and my cousin

Maleah would spend the night and I would try and do some sneaky stuff. I assumed aunt Charlene wouldn't know because she couldn't see me an she always knew. I never knew what strength was without sight until aunt Charlene.

When you think about some of your fears what comes to mind? Where do they stem from. What triggers them. Did you know the enemy takes those things that he knows gets under your skin to try and distract you in your spiritual walk. If we try and overcome some of those obstacles it would make things harder for the enemy to reach us.

Scare Tactic

"Who do you serve"

Terms:

- Scare tactic- a strategy intended to manipulate public opinion about a particular issue by arousing fear or alarm
- Fear- a feeling of anxiety concerning the outcome of something or the safety and well-being of someone.
- Obedient- complying or willing to comply with orders or requests; submissive to another's will.
- Trust- firm belief in the reliability, truth, ability, or strength of someone or something.
- Pray- address a solemn request or expression of thanks to a deity or other object of worship.   {Webster}

Daniel 3:1-6 & 12-18

Nebuchadnezzar the king made an image of gold, whose height was threescore cubits, and the breadth thereof sic cubits: he set it up in the plain of Dura, in the province if

Babylon. Then Nebuchadnezzar the king sent to gather together the princes, the governors, and the captains, the judges, the treasurers, the counsellors, the sheriffs, and all the rulers of the provinces, to come to the dedication of the image which Nebuchadnezzar the king has set up. Then the princes, the governors, and the captains, the judges, the treasures, the counsellors, the sheriffs, and all the rulers of the provinces, we gathered together unto the dedication of the image that Nebuchadnezzar had set up. Then an herald cried aloud, To you it is commanded, O people, nations, and languages, That at what time ye hear the sound of the cornet, flute, harp, sacbut, psaltery, dulcimer, and all kinds of musick, ye fall down and worship the golden image that Nebuchadnezzar the king hath set up: And whoso falleth not down and worshippeth shall the same hour be cast into the mist of a burning fiery furnace. -KJV

In this passage we see the king Nebuchadnezzar has took it upon himself to create a god. In doing so, he wanted everyone in the town to come and worship this new god that he had created and if you didn't your would be put to death instantly. Can you image living in this time where you were forced to do things you didn't want to do and if you rebelled it would cost you your life. How fun it that. None, at all. When I sat and pondered just these six versus I got to wandering how did all if this come about. Was the king just sitting in his chambers and he got bored and just randomly decided he'd create a god and force people to worship it. Was it something that he thought of just to do out of pure malaise just cause he can. I mean, what really brought this about.

Prior to reading chapter three. If you look back over in chapter two of the book of Daniel, you'd find that Nebuchadnezzar had a dream that no man could interpret. He couldn't remember the dream for himself so he began to put a demand on the people who stated they were magicians, astrologers, and all the other people that claimed to have power to interpret the dream for him. If you couldn't reveal unto him the dream and the meaning then you would be put to death. Why is death always the results of something with this king. He obviously didn't believe in second chances. But I am not here to judge or voice my opinions about him personally. Once the people realized they were unable to assist and all of their lives were endanger, there was found only one that could do such thing and that was Daniel.

(12-18)

'There are certain Jews whom thou hast set over the affairs of the province of Babylon, Shadrach, Meshach, and Abednego; these men, O king, have not regarded thee: they serve not the gods, nor worship the golden image which thou hast set up. Then Nebuchadnezzar in his rage and fury commanded to bring Shadrach, Meshach, and Abednego. Then they brought these men before the king. Nebuchadnezzar spake and said unto them, Is it true, O Shadrach, Meshack, and Abednego, do not ye serve my gods, nor worship the golden image which I have set up? Now if ye be ready that at what time ye hear the sound of the cornet, flute, harp, sackbut, psaltery, and dulcimer, and all kinds of musick, ye fall down and worship the image which I have made; well: but if ye worship not, ye shall be cast the same hour into the midst of a burning fiery furnace; and who is that God that shall deliver you out of my hands? Shadrach, Meshach, and Abednego, answered and said to the king, O Nebuchadnezzar, we are not careful to answer thee in this matter. If it be so, our God whom we serve is able to deliver us from the burning fiery furnace, and he will deliver us out of thine hand, O king. But if not, be it known unto thee, O king, that we will not serve thy gods, nor worship the golden image which thou hast set up.' -KJV

What kind of faith is this. What if we all had faith in 'I AM' the way that these fellows did. Can you imagine what kind of world this would be today if that level of faith existed. With this level of faith EVERYONE could walk on water cause I'm sure that would be the first thing everyone would want to attempt. I know I would. What can we say about these men? It can be said that they can't be threatened with death to do something that they didn't want to do and most certainly death wouldn't make them denounce their GOD. How many of us would be able to stand for our faith and risk it all if there was ever a time we had to choose. My mom has prepared me and my brother Adrian as far back as I can remember that the day would come and we would have to choose. Imagine being eight and your mom tells you, you might have to get your head chopped off for God. Who tells their kids that, but I'm grateful that she did.

But, what we've learned from this account referenced is that Shadrach, Meshach, and Abednego were all so secure and sure with their GOD that they wouldn't go against Him for nothing in this world. Don't let fear hinder you from standing up for what you believe or hinder you from doing anything that you want to do. If you read the rest of the story you'd find that their GOD came to their rescue and delivered them from the fiery pit. Isn't that amazing. Oh what a God we serve.

I want to leave you with a few encouraging scriptures to help you on your journey to overcome fear as I will study them as well:

John 16:33

'These things I have spoken unto you, that in me ye might have peace. In the world ye shall have tribulation: but be of good cheer; I have overcome the world.' -KJV

Leviticus 26:1

'Ye shall make you no idols nor graven image, neither rear you up a standing image, neither shall ye set up any image of stone in your land, to bow down unto it: for I am the Lord your God.' -KJV

I strongly feel you should draw your own conclusions on this one.

Proverbs 3:5-6

'Trust in the LORD with all thine heart; and lean not unto thine own understanding. In all thy ways acknowledge him, and he shall direct thy paths.' -KJV

When I think about trust and trusting others, I can honestly say due to past experiences I tend to be wary in doing so. It comes with such a high commitment and vulnerability that I get anxious just thinking about it. One things for sure, my God has never let me down. If I asked for something that He did not deliver, if I give Him time after I've calmed down. He always reveal to me why He didn't allow me to have it. Have you ever thought about something that you've prayed for and never got and after times passed you were grateful you didn't get it. Understand He is always working for us and not against us. Be sure to thank Him for being so possessive of you.

1 John 4:1-3

'Beloved, believe not every spirit, but try the spirits whether they are of God: because many false prophets are gone out into the world. Hereby know ye the Spirit of God: Every spirit that confesseth that Jesus Christ is come in the flesh is of God: And every spirit that confesseth not that Jesus Christ is come in the flesh is not of God: and this is that spirit of antichrist, whereof ye have heard that it should come; and even now already is it in the world.' -KJV

Ephesians 6:18

'Praying always with all prayer and supplication in the Spirit, and watching thereunto with all perseverance and supplication for all saints; -KJV

Blindfolded
"Believe or not"

Have you ever heard of the kids game 'Blind man blues'. If not, let me share a little bit with you regarding the concept of the game. You gather a group of friends in one room. In order for the game to be more appealing you don't want to exceed six participants depending on how large of a room you use. Using a scarf or whatever you want to use to blindfold one of the individuals, you cover their eyes so they can no longer see their surroundings. After this step is complete, you want to spin the person around eight to ten times, or typically enough to make them dizzy and then you let go. The object of the game for the person that is blindfolded is to try and find all of the people in the room. Whoever is tagged first will be the next person to be blind folded.

Terms

- Doubt- a feeling of uncertainty or lack of conviction.
- Blindfolded- deprive (someone) of sight by tying a piece of cloth around the head so as to cover the eyes.

Matthew 14:22-32

'And straightway Jesus constrained his disciples to get into a ship, and go before him unto the other side, while he sent the multitudes away. And when he had sent the multitudes away, he went up into a mountain apart to pray: and when the evening was come, he was there alone. But the ship was now in the midst of the sea, tossed with waves: for the wind was contrary. And in the fourth watch of the night Jesus went unto them, walking on the sea. And when the disciples saw him walking on the sea, they were troubled, saying, It is a spirit; and they cried out for fear. But straightway Jesus spake unto them, saying, Be of good cheer; it is I; be not afraid.' -KJV

Man, how awesome is this. Can you picture this view. Let me help you. Imagine you just left the biggest concert you've ever attended by your favorite artist. They feed you and then that artist tells you I'll meet you guys on the yacht after I finish handling some business. You don't ask no questions, you're excited, you don't question how they are going to meet you, all you know is they'll be there when you get there.

You and your crew are maxing and relaxing. You guys discuss what all went down at the show, you mention some of the highlights of the show and you go on and on for hours at a time in pure bliss. Then, you're hit with a hurricane and all of the fun has gone out the window cause now you're freaking out. Because you've been on the water for some time, it's pitch black. The only light you had was the light shinning from the moon and the stars, you're in the middle of the ocean.

Now use that same scenario and imagine you are one of the disciples and it's Jesus you're waiting on to meet you guys on the other side. Can you picture yourself in the mist of the storm. Can you see the boat rocking. Can you feel the heavy rain falling on your skin and your eyes are low trying to help tame the lines of the boat. Can you hear the thundering and see the lightening. Can you feel the rumble of the cracking that the thunder makes before it releases the next flash of light through the thick of the fog. The wind, do you feel the strength of the wind gusting. Now, look over to your right. Can you see a shaded figure of a man walking peacefully as to be taking a nice stroll on the beach passing by the boat unbothered by everything that you're currently experiencing. Yes, it's Jesus. He promised them he would meet them on the other side. He never specified how, he just stated he will.

(28-32)

'And Peter answered him and said, Lord, if it be thou, bid me come unto thee on the

water. And he said, Come. And when Peter was come down out of the ship, he walked on the water, to go to Jesus. But when he saw the wind boisterous, he was afraid; and beginning to sink, he cried, saying, Lord, save me. And immediately Jesus stretched forth his hand, and caught him, and said unto him, O thou of little faith, wherefore didst thou doubt? And when they were come into the ship, the wind ceased.' -KJV

How many of us are curious beyond reason. How many risk takers are out there. If you were Peter, would you have inquired of Jesus to bid you come? Speaking for myself and the state I'm in this day. I can't answer for the future Danielle, but as for the present Danielle. I would've been one of the eleven still in the boat. I would've been questioning the whole situation. I would've thought He was a ghost trying to get me. Honestly, I would've thought the worst of the worst. I don't blame the other eleven for the way they responded because they reacted the way anyone of us would have. I don't know if anyone is strong enough to admit they would have been amongst the eleven, but I won't get caught in a lie and say I would've been Peter. Own your truth, own where you are in your walk.

The biggest thing that stuck out to me was Peters strength. In this moment Peter was strong. Between that left foot being on the boat and that right foot touching the water that's strength. That's confidence. That's courage. That's faith. That's trust. That's reassurance that you know that you know that you know that you can walk on water to the Messiah. And in the midst of it all he had this rush of radical belief and was not afraid. Man, isn't that insane. I love it. And then, what did Jesus say to them 'be not afraid'. Geesh.

One thing that Peter did do that hindered him for making it completely to Christ without help, was the moment he took his eyes off of Him. However, don't miss the significance about what I'm going to say next. You can't do anything no matter what it is without the help of God.

Everything is done decent and in order. It was written for him to get distracted in order for their to be a need to be filled. Don't miss that. How many of us can admit to looking away a few times over the course of our lives up to this point? As you can see I am always willing to admit my shortcomings as an example because confession first comes before the deliverance. I'm not saying you have to be a open book. I choose this way for myself in order to help assist people in those same areas of weakness to see that they do have the ability to overcome as well.

One of the takeaways I would love for you to keep with you from this lesson is to believe and trust in the Lord no matter how radical. Be that radical Christian. Be that one that when God looks down and view the Earth in search of at least one individual that He knows loves Him and can always count on getting a smile from when He checks in. Let you name and address be that go to contact. Jesus is always on the mainline, tell Him what you want. And I can assure you, He will stand in proxy on your behalf to the Father and inquire that you be granted favor for your request. Shine on beautiful child of God.

James 1:6

'But let him ask in faith, nothing wavering. For he that wavereth is like a wave of the sea driven with the wind and tossed.' -KJV

Galatians 2:20

'I am crucified with Christ: nevertheless I live; yet not I, but Christ liveth in me: and the life which I now live in the flesh I live by the faith of the Son of God, who loved me and gave himself for me.' -KJV

Hebrew 11:6

'But without faith it is impossible to please him: for he that cometh to God must believe that he is, and that he is a rewarder of them that diligently seek him.' -KJV

Galatians 3:22

'But the scripture hath concluded all under sin, that the promise by faith of Jesus Christ might be given to them that believe.' -KJV

Danielle Walker

.....

RENEWED

There comes a time in our lives when we have a moment to ourselves and we find ourselves caught up in a daydream. We're not daydreaming of all the things we plan on doing in the future, but, daydreaming of all the things we've done in our past. We think about the fun times as far back as we can remember. We think about the bad situations we've endured and overcome. We think about the people that hurt us, and we ponder on the people we've wronged. There comes a time in our lives where we all sit and exhale and think. If you have not had this moment yet, I can assure you that you will. And for those of us who have can all admit it happens more often than we've come realize. What have you done to try and right some of the wrongs. What have you done to try and create more exciting memorable moments. Have you made any changes in your character since your last birthday. Have you grown in your financial mentality. Are you more of a giver than a receiver. Have you made efforts to strengthen your relationship with God. If all of your answers to these statements are 'no', don't let it bother you too much. We are all under construction.

Under Construction
"A work in progress"

Terms

- Construction- the style or method used in the building of something.
- Engineer- a skillful contriver or originator of something. {Webster}

Genesis 1:1-18

'In the beginning God created the heaven and the earth. And the earth was without form, and void; and darkness was upon the face of the deep. And the Spirit of God moved upon the face of the waters. And God said, Let there be light: and there was light. And God saw the light, that it was good: and God divided the light from darkness. And God called the light Day, and the darkness he called Night. And the evening and the morning were the first day.' -KJV

Upon reading these first five verses from the first chapter written in the bible. What have you concluded so far. So far I've come to see our God as the creator and He is creative. Where does my assumption of Him being creative stems from you ask. He had to first imagine a thing that He wanted before He thought to speak it into existence. Have you ever wondered if this was something He wrote out on like a Holy Scroll as He was coming up with these ideas? Am I the only one who thinks of these things. Like, do you think He actually writes Himself. Is there an appointed angel that writes for Him as He speaks and they toss out the papers or erase the ideas He don't like. Or, does the words from His idea just magically appear on a paper as He continues going through that creative process until He's satisfied with what He'd come up with. Is this something you ever wondered about or am I alone in this process of thinking. I don't want to ramble to much but I do want you to start thinking deeper. As a writer we go through this creative stage where we jot down a lot of ideas until we come up with something with enough substance that makes us smile.

The second thing I've noticed from just these few verses is that all God had to do was speak these things into existence. Do you know how awesome that is to be able to speak a thing and it manifests. We were also encouraged in Romans 4:17 to calleth those things which be not as though they were. That's why I try to watch what I say so I wont speak the wrong thing but only good things or nothing at all. So in one day God created a thing by speaking it and it's one of the most beautiful things none of us could've ever imagined ourselves. Ain't God good.

(6-10)

'And God said, Let there be a firmament in the midst of the waters, and let it divide the waters from the waters. And God made the firmament, and divided the waters which were under the firmament from the waters which were above the firmament: and it was so. And God called the firmament Heaven. And the evening and the morning were the second day. And God said, Let the waters under the heaven be gathered together unto one place, and let the dry land appear: and it was so. And God called the dry land Earth; and the gathering together of the waters called he Seas: and God saw that it was good.' - KJV

Have you ever had the chance to ride on a plane. It is the most beautiful sight you can ever see. I thought I enjoyed climbing mountains to look down and see the beauty, but the view from a plane is breath taking. It's nothing like you've ever seen or experienced ever before. Pictures really don't do the justice of actually seeing it with your own two eyes. When I first saw it, I was so amazed that I started thanking God for the opportunity and I imagined how He felt looking down every day at something so beautiful and breathtaking that He created. If you haven't had the opportunity to witness what our Creator has created, I encourage you to take a trip.

(11-18)

'And God said, Let the earth bring forth grass, the herb yielding seed, and the fruit tree yielding fruit after his kind, whose seed is in itself, upon the earth: and it was so. And the earth brought forth grass, and herb yielding seed after his kind, and the tree yielding fruit, whose seed was in itself, after his kind: and God saw that it was good. And the evening and the morning were the third day. And God said, Let there be lights in the firmament of the heaven to divide the day from the night; and let them be for signs, and for seasons, and for days, and years: And let them be for the lights in the firmament of the heaven to give light upon the earth: and it was so. And God made two great lights; the greater light to rule the day, and the lesser light to rule the night: he made the stars also. And God set them in the firmament of the heaven to give light upon the earth, And to rule over the day and over the night, and divide the light from the darkness: and God saw that it was good.' -KJV

I have a friend that has a garden in her backyard that she tends to. When I first saw it I was astonished at what she had hidden behind her gate in plain sight. No one knows about it expect her and the people she allows in her home. I couldn't believe it. I knew right then that was something I wanted to have for myself. I know it takes patience and a lot of hard work to maintain, but I'm still up for the challenge. Just knowing that I would have the ability to walk out of my home and snatch anything I wanted to eat straight from the vine still excites me. Being able to see what she planted allowed me to ability to expand my imagination of what God created here on this planet. Miles and miles of food. The beauty, the abundance, of what a sight.

If God can create all of these amazing things that no one else can create by speaking, what can't He do for you. We're all working to become a better us. Yes, we may stumble. Yes, we will fall. But as long as we never give up and we pick ourselves back up again, then everything will work out for our good. We didn't start out walking, we crawled first. We didn't start out on solid food, we had to be introduced to it after milk in a mush form. We aren't perfect Christians but as long as we keep working at it. Eventually we will get as close to perfect as man can with Gods help through Christ. So chin up champ and smile cause it ain't over yet.

Romans 10:9

'That if thou shalt confess with thy mouth the Lord Jesus, and shalt believe in thine heart that God hath raised him from the dead, thou shalt be saved.' -KJV

It's one thing to believe, but you have to speak it.

Acts 3:19

'Repent ye therefore, and be converted, that your sins may be blotted out, when the times of refreshing shall come from the presence of the Lord;' -KJV

Ask for forgiveness.

2 Timothy 2:15

'Study to show thyself approved unto God, a workman that needeth not to be ashamed, rightly dividing the wind of truth.' -KJV

Don't ashamed of God or the word of God. Take pride in your belief, your faith, and your walk with God. Keep your head in the book daily to promote growth in knowledge and in spirit. Your help and your strength cometh from the Lord, but how would you know what words to lean on if you've never read them. But, it's never too late to start.

Mark 16:15

'And he said unto them, Go ye into all the world, and preach the gospel to every creature.' -KJV

Shout it from the mountain tops, sing it in the depths of the valley. Tell your friends and share the good news with your family. Share with them the goodness of the Lord and bless them with the word. I remember one Christmas my mom didn't know what to get me and my brother and she gifted us a Bible with our name inscribed in them. Back then I was grateful for it, but as time went on I've come to know and feel this was the greatest gift anyone could've ever given me. And I still have it to this day. Just to share another personal story with you. I had a friend to get married back in 2018 and I didn't know what to get them as a gift and I went out and purchased them a Bible. It didn't take them long to figure out who gave it to them, but I'm happy I did because my friend told me she didn't have one. You never know how you can bless someone just by sharing. Sharing is caring.

The Gift

When attending a wedding it's customary that the guests present the bride and the groom with a gift in celebration. Pryor to a mother giving birth it's custom that her family and friends gather together for a baby shower to gift the baby. History has proven with every holiday and or special occasion, we tend to celebrate with some form of a gift exchange. But what do we consider the perfect gift. Some would argue the more expensive it is the better. Others would say it's the thought that count. What say you? Does the price of the item matter or the fact that someone thought enough of you to make s purchase for you. I have a tendency to not show up to the event if I can't present you with a gift. I know it's a bad habit to have, but I just don't like showing up empty handed. However, I encourage people to come to my gatherings empty handed or not.

Terms

- Gift- a thing given willingly to someone without payment; a present.
- King- the male ruler of an independent state, especially one who inherits the position by right of birth.   {Webster}

Isaiah 7:6-12

'Let us go up against Judah, and vex it, and let us make a breach therein for us, and set a king in the midst of it, even the son of Tabeal: Thus saith the Lord GOD, It shall not stand, neither shall it come to pass. For the head of Syria is Damascus, and the head of Damascus is Rezin; and within threescore and five years shall Ephraim be broken, that it be not a people. And the head of Ephrain is Samaria, and the head of Samaria is Remaliah's son. If ye will not believe, surely ye shall not be established. Moreover, the LORD spake again unto Ahaz, saying, Ask thee a sign of the LORD they GOD; ask it either in the depth, or in the height above. But Ahaz said, I will not ask, neither will I tempt the LORD.' -KJV

In these few versus we see the Lord sent Isaiah to meet Ahaz and warn him of the other cities preparing to come against Judah. But He assures him that they wont prevail in attempt and to not fear. Then we see that God gave Ahaz an opportunity to ask of Him any question he wanted, but Ahaz didn't want to tempt God by asking.

(13-16)

'And he said, Hear ye now, O house of David; It is a small thing for you to weary men, but will ye weary my God also? Therefore the Lord himself shall give you a sign; Behold, a virgin shall conceive, and bear a son, and shall call his name Immanuel. Butter and honey shall he eat, that he may know to refuse the evil, and choose the good. For before the child shall know to refuse the evil, and choose good, the land that thou abhorrest shall be forsaken of both her kings.' -KJV

Here we see that that people were told that God was going to give the people a sign and the sign would be a child. How did we get to this point. In the beginning chapters of Isaiah, God was not pleased with the people. It got so bad that He stopped receiving their offering and stopped listening to their prayers. Why was He angry? Because they starting rebelling against Him and the sin had become so great that the sacrifices were no longer acceptable for covering.

Wanting to spare those who still believed and abided by His commandments. God took it upon himself to offer a gift to the people that would not only give them the ability to pray to Him again, but save them as well.

Luke 1:26-31

'And in the sixth month the angel Gabriel was sent from God unto a city of Galilee, named Zazareth, To a virgin espoused to a man whose name was Joseph, of the house of David; and the virgin's name was Mary. And the angel came in unto her, and said, Hail, thou that art highly favoured, the Lord is with thee: blessed art thou among women. And when she saw him, she was troubled at his saying, and cast in her mind what manner of salutation this should be. And the angel said unto her, Fear not, Mary:

for thou hast found favour with God. And, behold, thou shalt conceive in thy womb, and bring forth a son, and shalt call his name JESUS.' -KJV

Lets stop for a few minutes and just take in all that we've just read. God favored Mary and He planned on using her to birth the Gift into this world. Can you imagine being Mary and having an angel come and tell you that you are going to have a baby. I wonder if she knew what he meant. Like did she know that Joseph wasn't going to actually touch her and that God was going to bless her womb. Can you imagine being her. Would you have freaked out or would you have been calm and welcoming. Would you have thought the angel was crazy? Did she recognize him as an angel? I know that's a lot to think about, but I just want you to try and place yourself in that day and time. When reading don't think as though you're reading history as it was, try reading as if it is present and you're in the midst.

(32-38)

'He shall be great, and shall be called the Son of the Highest: and the Lord God shall give unto him the throne of his father David: And he shall reign over the house of Jacob for ever; and of his kingdom there shall be no end. Then said Mary unto the angel, How shall this be, seeing I know not a man? And the angel answered and said unto her, The Holy Ghost shall come upon thee, and the power of the Highest shall overshadow thee: therefore also that holy thing which shall be born of thee shall be called the Son of God. And, behold, thy cousin Elisabeth, she hath also conceived a son in her old age: and this is the sixth month with her, who was called barren.' -KJV

Placing yourself back in Mary's shoes and having an 'angel' of all people an 'angel' tell you of all the things your child will become and have, doesn't that spark a sense of excitement and joy in you. I know in this day if the Lord sent an angel to tell me all of these amazing things about my future child I'd start crying and be so happy and so proud to be it's mother. You couldn't tell me nothing. When that baby finally come I know I would speak positive things to him everyday and just smoother him with kisses and pour on the extreme extra love. Because I would know without a doubt that my baby would grow up to be someone great. Not saying I wouldn't do that to my regular children but you know what I mean.

Matthew 1:18-21

'Now the birth of Jesus Christ was on this wise: When as his mother Mary was espoused to Joseph, before they came together, she was found with child of the Holy Ghost. Then Joseph her husband, being a just man, and not willing to make her a public example, was minded to put her away privily. But while he thought on these things, behold, the angel of the Lord appeared unto him in a dream, saying, Joseph, thou son of David, fear not to take unto thee Mary thy wife: for that which is conceived in her is of the Holy Ghost. And she shall bring forth a son, and thou shalt call his name JESUS: for he shall save his people from their sins.' -KJV

WOW! What a burden to be born with to know that you were born to die for people you know and don't know. But I'm grateful that Jesus didn't see it as a burden and was willing to make that sacrifice so I too myself could have an opportunity to live, serve, worship, and reign with my Heavenly Father and a right to the tree of life. I can just shout off of that alone. What greater love. What greater gift. The Ultimate gift.

Luke 2:1-6

'AND IT came to pass in those days, that there went out a decree from Caesar Augustus, that all the world should be taxed. (And this taxing was first made when Cyrenius was governor of Syria.) And all went to be taxed, every one into his own city. And Joseph also went up from Galilee, out of the city of Nazareth, into Judaea, unto the

city of David, which is called Bethlehem; (because he was of the house and lineage of David:) To be taxed with Mary his espoused wife, being great with child. And so it was, that, while they were there, the days were accomplished that she should be delivered.' - KJV

We've now come to the point to where it's time for Jesus to be born.

(7-14)

'And she brought forth her firstborn son, and wrapped him in swaddling clothes, and laid him in a manger; because there was no room for them in the inn. And there were in the same country shepherds abiding in the field, keeping watch over their flock by night. And, lo, the angel of the Lord came upon them, and the glory of the Lord shone round about them: and they were sore afraid. And the angel said unto them, Fear not: for, behold, I bring you good tidings of great joy, which shall be to all people. For unto you is born this day in the city of David a Saviour, which is Christ the Lord. And this shall be a sign unto you; Ye shall find the babe wrapped in swaddling clothes, lying in a manger. And suddenly there was with the angel a multitude of the heavenly host praising God, and saying, Glory to God in the highest, and on earth peace, good will toward men.' - KJV

Have you ever heard that song 'I love you forever' by Tye Tribbett? If not, I encourage you to go listen to it. What's significant about it, is that's the song I imagined when I read the part about all of the heavenly host joined in with the angel to praise God and sing. Man, take five minutes away from your reading and just get into that song. Let's create an atmosphere of praise and welcome the Lord into your space.

You've just witness and heard about the birth of Christ. You've just joined in unison with the angels and every being created in heaven in gratefulness and praise for the gift God gave man (you). How amazing does that feel? How blessed do you feel now that you've come into the full realization that your creator love you enough to take the time to create a gift so special for you that would wipe away all of your sins. To know that your debts have been paid and the process started through Jesus's birth. That's deep.

John 14:6

'Jesus said unto him, I am the way, the truth, and the life: no man cometh unto the Father, but by me.' -KJV

DECIDE

When we open our eyes every morning we take no thought of it. We tend to get up and start our morning routines. Whether that be to use the bathroom, start our kettle for coffee, or walk in our kids room to wake them for school. Either way we do it without thinking about our actions we just take action. What if we started thinking more before we acted. Would you agree that this could potentially be a better world to live in or do you think nothing would change. I guess we would have to assume that everyone would be making great decisions in order for this planet to become better right. Even I know that's asking a bit much, but I digress.

When we fall asleep, we tend to assume that we are going to awake the next day. But have you ever considered that there is a possibility that you may not. During those early hours of the morning there is still activity outside of your home. People are driving up and down your street, others are having our with their friends, some are coming and going to work, and you have neighbors that can be up arguing in the house next to you. All of these outside factors can affect whether or not your eyes open when the sun rises and not to mention your heath. I'm not mentioning these thing to scare you, but I want to encourage you to think a different way.

Tomorrow

"Check your connection"

Terms

- Tomorrow- the day after today.
- Decide- come to a resolution in the mind as a result of consideration.
- Choice- an act of selecting or making a decision when faced with two or more possibilities.
- Procrastination- the action of delaying or postponing something
- Times up- the period of time allowed for something is ended.

{Webster}

"Boast not thyself of tomorrow; for thou knowest not what a day may bring forth." -Proverbs 27:1

"Watch therefore, for ye know neither the day nor the hour wherein the Son of man cometh." -Matthew 25:13

Genesis 6:5-7

'And God saw that the wickedness of man was great in the earth, and that every imagination of the thoughts of his heart was only evil continually. And it repented the LORD that he had made man on the earth, and it grieved him at his heart. And the LORD said, I will destroy man whom I have created from the face of the earth; both man, and beast, and the creeping thing, and the fowls of the air; for it repenteth me that I have made them.' -KJV

I want to first start by saying oh how I love the Lord. I am personally grateful that He later decided to save Noah and spare the earth fully so I could have this opportunity that I have right now to share with you the goodness of our God. I think this is a moment in history that we truly take for granted of the fact that there was a time when none of us would've ever made it to this life. We have proof here that God regretted creating us. The people had become so evil and disobedient that it reached a level to where it hurt God deeply for the thought of making us. I NEVER want Him to ever feel that way again. That hurts me knowing that we hurt Him that bad to make Him say he's going to destroy everything. Just think about it.

(8-14)

'But Noah found grace in the eyes of the LORD. These are the generation of Noah: Noah was a just man and perfect in his generations, and Noah walked with God. And Noah begat three sons, Shem, Ham, and Japheth. The earth also was corrupt before God, and the earth was filled with violence. And God looked upon the earth, and, behold, it was corrupt; for all flesh had corrupted his way upon the earth. And God said unto Noah, The end of all flesh is come before me; for the earth is filled with violence through them; and, behold, I will destroy them with the earth. Make thee an ark of gopher wood; rooms shalt thou make in the ark, and shalt pitch it within and without with pitch.' -KJV

Thank God for grace. If you take some time to read Genesis chapter one through six. You will find that the angels had become envious of the men on earth and started sleeping with the women. After this happened the children that were born because of this act were known as the giants and God never intended for these things to take place. Consider all of the things that's happening now in our day compared to what happened back then, we can conclude our generation maybe the worst yet. The only difference between then and now is the fact that we have a bit more leniency which is

Christ that we tend to take for granted knowingly and unknowingly. What if God never intended on recreating the world after his first thought to destroy everything. I'm so glad He found one in the mist of all of those people and decided to spare him and give him a survival plan.

One thing that I can share with you that I've learned is whenever I've found myself in a tight spot and I went to God in prayer for help. He always have made a way for me to come out of the situation I was in. Even down to a relationship. If I liked someone and I started getting my flirt on and it never worked out in my favor. After time had passed, God would reveal unto me why His answer was 'no'. I thank God that he loves me enough to say 'no' to me when he knows it's for my good. Have you ever been through a similar situation. Maybe a job you thought you wanted but never got and found out later on that you were better off without it. Sometimes it's the simplest things we miss out on as counting as one of our blessings.

1 Thessalonians 5:1-2

'BUT OF the times and the seasons, brethren, ye have no need that I write unto you. For yourselves know perfectly that the day of the Lord so cometh as a thief in the night.' - KJV

No one has to tell you that God is coming back, because this is something you already know. You've been told and you've been warned since the first day of your understanding. No one can ever say that they were never told that God was coming back to judge the world. Whether you believed them or not is on you, but you were told.

Matthew 24:44

'Therefore be ye also ready: for in such an hour as ye think not the Son of man cometh.' -

KJV

Jesus is warning the people (us) to be ready, because he can come back at any point in time and you don't want to miss him when he comes. It would be when we least expect it. Therefore, if you're always ready you won't get left behind.

1 Thessalonians 5:11-18

'Wherefore comfort yourselves together, and edify one another, even as also ye do. And we beseech you, brethren, to know them which labour among you, and are over you in the Lord, and admonish you; And to esteem them very highly in love for their work's sake. And be at peace among yourselves. Now we exhort you, brethren, warn them that are unruly, comfort the feebleminded, support the weak, be patient toward all men. See that none render evil for evil unto any man; but ever follow that which is good, both among yourselves, and to all men. Rejoice evermore. Pray without ceasing. In every thing give thanks: for this is the will of God in Christ Jesus concerning you.' -KJV

You have to know the people that are around you. You have to know who's side they're on. Whether it be for God or for the devil. One of the reasons it's important that you know, because you need to have a clear understanding of who's for you and who's against you. Everyone that smiles in your face does not wish you well and every one you may call friend is not your friend. If there's someone around you and they are being mean or nasty to someone else then you should encourage them to be kind. You don't want to be considered as being apart of the problem. If things were to get out of hand and the authorities get involved. They would take you in for booking as well because you would be consider an accomplice. When you were really just an innocent bystander.

In everything you do give thanks. Get in the habit of thanking God for everything. Even if you get a free unexpected meal at your job, shout thank you Jesus with a heart of gratitude. Feel meals don't come around that often, but oh when they do. I be like shouting John. The first thing that comes flying out of my mouth is 'look at God', and I be loud. Ain't no shame in my game. I give credit where credit is due. You got to put a praise on that thanks. Pray daily. Even if it's just for five seconds, it will grow with time. Share the word. You never know who may need a bit of encouragement and your smile.

Don't wait until tomorrow to give your life to Christ, tomorrow might be to late. Let go and let God. Let God have his way.

My Words Have Power
"Are you speaking blessings or curses"

<u>**Terms**</u>

- Speak- say something in order to convey information, an opinion, or a feeling.

- Blessing- God's favor and protection.

- Curse- a solemn utterance intended to invoke a supernatural power to inflict harm or punishment on someone or something.

- Mindful- conscious or aware of something.

- Guidance- advice or information aimed at resolving a problem or difficulty, especially as given by someone in authority.

- Wait- stay where one is or delay action until a particular time or until something else happens.   {Webster}

Have you ever said something you weren't supposed to say growing up and your mom tells you to watch your mouth. Those may not have been her exact words but you know what I mean. Have you ever said something to someone in anger that hurt their feelings and it was so bad that you felt bad and stated that you didn't mean to say it. I know we all can say that someone has said something to us simultaneously or even in constructive criticism and it still touched a nerve for us in the same way. How many times have you heard someone say that they were proud of you? Have you ever said that to someone? How did it make you feel? Did it give you a feeling of gratitude and made you want to accomplish more so you could receive more accolades. Now, think about this in a spiritual context. You have the ability to uplift or tear down someone's spiritual being knowingly and unknowingly. And you can speak things over yourself intentionally and unintentionally. Lets see what the word has to say about the power of the tongue.

Matthew 12:31-33

'Wherefore I say unto you, All manner of sin and blasphemy shall be forgiven unto men: but the blasphemy against the Holy Ghost shall not be forgiven unto men. And whosoever speaketh a word against the Son of man, it shall be forgiven him: but whosoever speaketh against the Holy Ghost, it shall not be forgiven him, neither in this world, neither in the world to come. Either make the tree good, and his fruit good; or else make the tree corrupt, and his fruit corrupt: for the tree is known by his fruit.' -KJV

Here Jesus is having a conversation with the Pharisees giving warning unto them. Earlier in the text they were having dialog about what should and shouldn't be done on the sabbath. The people were trying to find reasons to support their desire to destroy him. Therefore, they started nitpicking. However, with every accusation Jesus gave a rebuttal for a solution.

As you read deeper into chapter twelve you'd start noticing Jesus begins to give warnings. Here he clearly tells the people to be mindful of what they say, because if they speak ill of the Holy Ghost they won't be forgiven. We've grown accustom to having the ability to repent for things we've done repeatedly with the assurance that if we repent everything will be forgiven. Yet, I honestly believe there are limits to that as well. To do a thing and learn it's wrong and ask forgiveness is forgiven. But, I believe if you keep doing it over and over and over knowing that it's wrong and you keep doing it because you know the Lord will forgive you. I feel at some point that's kind of like mocking God. Especially if you're just doing it cause you can. Now, if it's something that has become a habit that you are trying to break. I think He may be a little bit more understanding in that type of situation.

When you think about what Jesus could have meant about speaking blasphemy against the Holy Ghost. I think he meant like cursing God and using His name in vain. That's definitely a big no, no. How can you feel at ease even doing such a thing. I wouldn't feel safe. I know I've seen a few television shows here recently and I won't quote any names. Where the actors have said some damning things against the Lord in the name of acting. Now, me personally. I don't care what you say or what you do, you couldn't pay me enough to do anything as crazy as that. When I heard it. I turned the station and no longer watched those shows. I refuse to be a partaker of that mess. If I'd continued to watch it would've been as if I condoned what was happening and you never know. That could possibly be an issue for you when judgement day comes.

Jesus says either make the tree good or corrupt. Meaning to my own understanding you can either speak life and do good deeds, or speak bad and live a unfruitful life.

(34-37)

'O generation of vipers, how can ye, being evil, speak good things? For out of the

abundance of the heart the mouth speaketh. A good man out of the good treasure of the heart bringeth forth good things: and an evil man out of the evil treasure bringeth for evil things. But I say unto you, That every idle word that men shall speak, they shall give account thereof in the day of judgement. For by thy words thou shalt be justified, and by thy words thou shalt be condemned.' -KJV

Jesus is saying how can you being a person of ill will and always doing mischief speak something positive to someone when your heart is corroded. You can say it but nothing is going to become of your words. But, if someone who's heart is pure and have an abundance of joy and love speak the same positivity into someone those things will begin to manifest into that individuals life. In verse thirty-six Jesus begins to warn us that no matter what, whatever you shall speak you will have to answer for it in judgement. Therefore, lets all strive to be more conscious of what we say this day moving forward.

Proverbs 18-21

'Death and life are in the power of the tongue: and they that love it shall eat the fruit thereof.' -KJV

You have the ability to speak good things in your life and the ability to hinder your own growth and prosperity. We are who we say we say.

Ephesians 4:29

'Let no corrupt communication proceed out of your mouth, but that which is good to the use of edifying, that it may minister grace unto the hearers.' -KJV

Let's make an effort to stop speaking negatively about our friends and our family members. If we try to make an effort to find those unique qualities to speak about, then maybe we'd start seeing a change in those people and in ourselves as well.

Proverbs 12:18

'There is that speaketh like the piercings of a sword: but the tongue of the wise is heath.' - KJV

Meaning you can say something that can hurt the soul of someone. You have the potential to say something that can make someone feel insecure about themselves or even in a relationship you can make them feel less than. But why do that when you wouldn't want someone to do that to you. You also have the ability to say something so uplifting and encouraging that can give someone confidence to try something they felt like they could never do. Or, make them feel like they are special, needed, and desired. Aim to give out smiles and not frowns.

Matthew 7:7-8

'Ask, and it shall be given unto you; seek, and ye shall find; knock, and it shall be opened unto you: For every one that asketh receiveth; and he that seeketh findeth; and to him that knocketh it shall be opened.'

Psalms 27:14

'Wait on the LORD: be of good courage, and he shall strengthen thine heart: wait, I say, on the LORD.'

BLESSED

Did you know you are loved. If you didn't know, let me be the first to tell you. I love you. I know you may be thinking how can she love me and she never met me. She don't even know what I look like. She don't know what I've been through or even what I like. Listen up, it doesn't matter. I love you anyway. It's a choice and I choose to love you, just like you've chose to love our God. Every morning you open your eyes, consider yourself blessed. When you inhale, consider yourself blessed. When you stretch your foot over the cliff of your bed, you're blessed. When you stand and stretch yourself without help or even with help, still, consider yourself blessed. Being blessed isn't always monetary or something given to you as a gift. Blessings are the things we take for granted.

Trust in the Lord

<u>Terms</u>

- Trust- firm belief in the reliability, truth, ability, or strength of someone or something.
- Courage- the ability to do something that frightens one.

- Bravery- courageous behavior or character.

{Webster}

Putting your trust in someone takes a lot of courage. Especially if you've had your trust misused before. They say trust is earned. While others believe it's given automatically until you do something to no longer be worth trusting. Personally, the way my trust is set it. It can go either way for me. First off, it takes me forever to start talking to you. I may do the occasional good morning and goodbye, but that's not personal. I consider that well-mannered. I tend to watch the person actions and interactions with others before I feel it's safe to even do more than just a greeting and that process alone can take years. I've come to learn through experience that you can't be so trusting. However, you still have those individuals you meet that you trust immediately by choice.

Exodus 16-1-3

'And they took their journey from Elim, and all the congregation of the children of Israel came unto the wilderness of Sin, which is between Elim and Sinai, on the fifteenth day of the second month after their departing out of the land of Egypt. And the whole congregation of the children of Israel murmured against Moses and Aaron in the wilderness: And the children of Israel said unto them, Would to God we had died by the hand of the LORD in the land of Egypt, when we sat by the flesh pots, and when we did eat bread to the full; for ye have brought us forth into the wilderness, to kill this whole assembly with hunger.' -KJV

After being freed from slavery, God used Moses to lead the children of Israel over to the land that was promised them. However, on their journey they began to complain because they were hungry.

(4-7)

'Then said the LORD unto Moses, Behold, I will rain bread from heaven for you; and the people shall go out and gather a certain rate every day, that I may prove them, whether they will walk in my law, or no. And it shall come to pass, that on the sixth day that they shall prepare that which they bring in; and it shall be twice as much as they gather daily. And Moses and Aaron said unto all the children of Israel, At even, then ye shall know that the LORD hath brought you out from the land of Egypt: And in the morning, then ye shall see the glory of the LORD; for that he hearth your murmurings against the LORD: and what are we, that ye murmur against us?' -KJV

Have you ever been in a place to where someone said they were going to do something for you and you got frustrated with them because they didn't do it in a timely manner that you expected it to happen. What happened in that situation? Did you begin to speak ill of the person or did you loose trust in anything they may say to you moving forward? From my own personal account I can admit to having trust issues with people who tell me they are going to do something and then don't do it at all. However, that's not the case here.

What we began to see is the people no longer trusting God's word. He told them that he was going to deliver them from bondage and He did. He told them that He was going to move them over to the land that was promised their forefathers and on their journey they would be taken care of. At what point did they not think that they wouldn't eat. Instead of looking at their current circumstance they could've considered the thing that they thought was never possible would be made possible. If the Lord can part the sea, then surely He can provide them something to eat.

I truly believe if they allowed God the room to do what He does best without all of the complaining they did. They would've made it over into the promise land. Patience is a virtue so I've heard. There's definitely levels to patience's. If you're waiting on something that you've prayed about that hasn't come through yet, don't murmur about it. I encourage you to trust the Lord and that He has your best interest in mind. And if it's something that you never obtain. Just know that He kept it from you to bless you with something better. Be encouraged my friend.

Psalm 56:4

'In God I will praise his word, in God I have put my trust; I will not fear what flesh can do unto me.' -KJV

In everything you do trust God. Don't doubt Him for nothing. If you ask a thing, give it time to manifest. There is peace in waiting.

Proverbs 3:5-6

'Trust in the LORD with all thine heart; and lean not unto thine own understanding. In all thy ways acknowledge him, and he shall direct thy paths.' -KJV

If you find yourself in a place of confusion and you don't know which way is up or down, go to God in prayer. Growing up as a kid I had issues with remaining focus. My mom would fuss at me about staying focus when I would get off track in school because she knew it had something to do with a boy. I was a little hopeless romantic, but I digress. What I've found now that I'm older and I notice that I'm starting to stray. I ask God to help me focus and to help strengthen my discipline. Discipline is key.

Jeremiah 17: 7-8

'Blessed is the man that trusteth in the LORD, and whose hope the LORD is. For he shall be as a tree planted by the waters, and that spreadeth out her roots by the river, and

shall not see when hear cometh, but her leaf shall be green; and shall not be careful in the year of drought, neither shall cease from yielding fruit.' -KJV

Psalm 9:10

'And they that know thy name will put their trust in thee: for thou, LORD, hast not forsaken them that seek thee.' -KJV

Psalm 46:10

'Be still, and know that I am God: I will be exalted among the heathen, I will be exalted in the earth.' -KJV

The Tables Are Turning

"Don't allow your enemies to cost you your destiny"

Terms

- Ask- request (someone) to do or give something.
- Anticipation- the action of anticipating something; expectation or prediction.
- Manifestation- an event, action, or object that clearly shows or embodies something, especially a theory or an abstract idea.
- Mock- tease or laugh at in a scornful or contemptuous manner.
- Complain- express dissatisfaction or annoyance about something.

{Webster}

1 Samuel 1: 4-7

'And when the time was that Elkanah offered, he gave to Peninnah his wife, and to all her sons and her daughters, portions: But unto Hannah he gave a worthy portion; for he loved Hannah: but the LORD had shut up her womb. And her adversary also provoked

her sore, for to make her fret, because the LORD had shut up her womb. And as he did so year by year, when she went up to the house of the LORD, so she provoked her; therefore she wept, and did not eat.' -KJV

Let's dive into this text. This is the story of Elkanah. A man with two wives. One was barren and one was fruitful. Which meant one could have children and the other one couldn't. During the duration of their marriage the wife that could have children Peninnah, taunted Hannah for her lack thereof. Not only did Hannah have to endure the pains of being taunted by Peninnah for not having children. She also had to deal with the fact that she didn't get a big portion for a sacrifice because she was by herself year after year.

One day Elkanah noticed Hannah stopped eating and she was crying and he went and asked her what was bothering her. However, still willing to endure the hand that was dealt her and not complain about all that she was dealing with emotionally. Hannah refused to complain by telling him and she went to God in prayer instead, where she met a priest by the name of Eli. Let's put a pin in the story for now and I'll share with you what happened a little later in the text.

I thought this story would be a good example of what some of us endure day to day. Maybe not in the same context, but we do deal with issues that cause us to feel less than at times. We also deal with people on a day to day aspect that mock us for something we don't have or we mock them. Have you ever been mocked for something that was out of your control? I want you take a moment outside of yourself and place yourself in Hannah's shoes. In that day in time you were blessed by the children that you had. It was known that the first son born was the blessing. What did God command us to do? Be fruitful and multiply right. Therefore, if a woman wasn't able to produce, they were frowned upon.

Now that you've placed yourself in her shoes. Imagine all of the family gatherings, parties, and outings that you and your husband and other wife attended every year. Everyone that you know brings their kids and their grandkids and usually the topic of the women's conversations at these events are centered around the children. They complain about the sleepless nights, they talk about school, and they talk about the issues of feeding. However, you (Hannah) are off in a corner because you can't relate to what they are speaking about. You see your husband engaged with the other men and you see Peninnah laughing with the other wives and then in a moment you see one of the children run away from Peninnah into Elkanah arms. How would that make you feel.

I know speaking from my own personal account. If I was in this situation, I would feel as though my husband didn't love me as much as he loved Peninnah. I would feel as though our bond isn't as strong because we didn't share anything with each other outside of a commitment in marriage. I know it would make me feel insecure and question why he stayed with me and I couldn't produce for him. I would feel like a burden. And to add the fact that Peninnah was rubbing this in my face every chance she got. We can all agree that there would come a point of being tired of being sick and tired right.

However, what I love about the decision Hannah decided to make when she came to her breaking point was beyond wise. Instead of complaining to her husband about something that he couldn't do anything about. She went to the source. The one who can turn her situation upside down. The one who can open her womb with the speaking of His word. She went to pray. I know I would've prayed after I laid the smack down on Peninnah, but I digress.

While in the mist of praying and pouring out her sorrows to the LORD. Hannah made a vow that if the LORD granted her request, she would give the child over to Him. And I believe because of her vow, God granted Hannah her desire. Not only did she conceive, but her first born was a boy. Guess what his name was, Samuel. Hannah kept her promise and God blessed her with even more children after that. Lets look at this situation from another point of view. What if Hannah didn't go to God for assistance and she took matters into her own hands. What if she retaliated in a negative way against Peninnah and ended up in a situation that would cause her to lose her husband and her freedom. There wouldn't be room for God to come in and work a miracle for them to share with their peers as a testimony.

Now, what situation have you been dealing with that has become to much for you to bare that you haven't yet given over to God to fix for you. Here is your opportunity to let it go and give it up. Place it in His hands and allow Him to breathe on it and give you a testimony. I know it's easier said than done because we all want to feel as though we can handle anything that comes our way. But let me be the first to say 'I can't handle nothing on my own'. I am a full dependent of Christ. I said if Jesus could file taxes he can write my name down and get a huge deduction, because I go to Him for EVERYTHING. Even on things I don't want to bring to him, I still give it up. I haven't always been this way, I had to grow into this state. You have to come to a point where you realize there's no point of getting mad at something you can't control or change. Most times denial is for your benefit and for God to get the glory.

Notables

❖ (Matthew 20:16) *'So the last shall be first, and the first last: for many be called, but few chosen.'* -KJV

❖ (Mark 11:24) *'Therefore I say unto you, What things soever ye desire, when ye pray, believe that ye receive them, and ye shall have them.'* -KJV

❖ (John 15:7) *'If ye abide in me, and my words abide in you, ye shall ask what ye will, and it shall be done unto you.'* -KJV

❖ (John 14:13-15) *'And whatsoever ye shall ask in my name, that will I do, that the Father may be glorified in the Son. If ye shall ask any thing in my name, I will do it. If ye love me, Keep my commandments.'* -KJV

\<Manifestation>

1 Samuel 1:19-20

'And they rose up in the morning early, and worshipped before the LORD, and returned, and came to their house to Ramah: and Elkanah knew Hannah his wife; and the LORD remembered her. Wherefore it came to pass, when the time was come about after Hannah had conceived, that she bare a son, and called his name Samuel, saying, Because I have asked him of the LORD.' -KJV

God never breaks a promise. If He say He's going to do something for you. You can bet everything you have that it's going to come to pass. When you find yourself in a place of doubt, there will always be a witness to come and remind you of what was said. Meaning, someone that you've never met may come and tell you that you are going to have something that only God could have told them for them to know. This typically takes place in church. Even though you already know it, it's confirmation to ease you in your wait to not get weary.

As we review the text referenced above. God remembered Hannah and the promise He made to fulfill and she conceived. Imagine how excited she was after all those years of suffering and finally getting what she desired most. I know she cried. As a woman when you become overjoyed sometimes there are no words, just tears. Only tears can express the gratitude you feel because the words don't exist. Think about the shock that came from Peninnah. Not only did Hannah and Elkanah conceive Samuel. They had more children thereafter. Oh how the tables turn.

One of the lessons I've learned from this story is nothing is guaranteed unless God say that it is. You can have something one day and lose it the next. Be kind too those that are less fortunate because the tables can always turn in their favor. I really hope you've enjoyed the story of Elkanah, Peninnah, and Hannah. It's a story not commonly shared throughout the churches, but there are significant revelations that can be revealed from within it. Just ask.

SURRENDER

We watch and we wait, until there's no debate. And we recognize you're already here. I really wanted to make that statement to get your mind in a state of acknowledging God is already in your mist. No matter where you go or what you do, He will always be there with you. One thing I really love about God is that He gives us 'choice'. He will never force himself on you and He will never make you do something you don't want to do. Unless, He's given you a task to complete and you refuse to do it. Then, that's a whole other conversation. It's easier to obey then disobey.

Go Forth

"Voluntarily or Involuntarily"

<u>**Terms:**</u>

- Stubbornness- dogged determination not to change ones attitude or position on something.

- Rebellion- an act of violence or open resistance to an established government or ruler.

- Innocent Bystander- a viewer, watcher, on looker, a guiltless witness of a crime.

- Prepare- make (something) ready for use or consideration.

{Webster}

Jonah 1:1-3

'Now the word of the LORD came unto Jonah the son of Amittai, saying, Arise, go to Nineveh, that great city, and cry against it; for their wickedness is come up before me. But Jonah rose up to flee unto Tarshish from the presence of the LORD, and went down to Joppa; and he found a ship going to Tarshish: so he paid the fare thereof, and went down into it, to go with them unto Tarshish from the presence of the LORD.' -KJV

At the beginning of this text we witness Jonah receiving a message from the Lord to deliver to the people of Nineveh. Because of fear, he decided not to relay the message and run instead. Has God ever asked you to do something in the past or present that you refused to do?

4-7

'But the LORD sent out a great wind into the sea, and there was a mighty tempest in the sea, so that the ship was like to be broken. Then the mariners were afraid, and cried every man unto his god, and cast forth wares that were in the ship into the sea, to lighten it of them. But Jonah was gone down into the sides of the ship; and he lay, and was fast asleep. So the shipmaster came to him, and said unto him, What meanest thou, O sleeper? arise, call upon thy God, if so be that God will think upon us, that we perish not. And they said every one to his fellow, Come, and let us cast lots, that we may know for whose cause this evil is upon us. So they cast lots, and the lot fell upon Jonah.' -KJV

We've established that God gives us choice, unless it's something He really wants us to do. This is a good example of one of those things where we would be better off doing what it is He asks. Instead of having to make

Him make us do it. Because of Jonah's rebellion, God took action to make the place he resided uncomfortable. Not only did his rebellion affect him, it affected everyone that was around him.

8-12

'Then said they unto him, Tell us, we pray thee, for whose cause this evil is upon us; What is thine occupation? and whence comest thou? what is thy country? and of what people art thou? And he said unto them, I am an Hebrew; and I fear the LORD, the God of heaven, which hath made the sea and the dry land. Then were the men exceedingly afraid, and said unto him. Why hast thou done this? For the men knew that he fled from the presence of the LORD, because he had told them. Then said they unto him, What shall we do unto thee, that the sea may be calm unto us? for the sea wrought, and was tempestuous. And he said unto them, take me up, and cast me forth into the sea; so shall the sea be calm unto you: for I know that for my sake this great tempest is upon you.' - KJV

When things around us become chaotic. We tend to know what we've done to bring that chaos into our lives. Jonah knew his disobedience was the cause of the storm. And he knew what it would take for it to cease and the other sailors to survive. I want you to take a minute to reflect and ask yourself have you ever done something and it was time to reap the punishment and the people around you had to suffer through with you? Or, have you ever got a whipping for something that someone else did. All because your mom decided that everyone that was involved was going to get it. If that wasn't one of the worst innocent bystander incidents as a child, I don't know what else could've been.

13-17

'Nevertheless the men rowed hard to bring it to the land; but they could not: for the sea

wrought, and was tempestuous against them. Wherefore they cried unto the LORD, and said, We beseech thee, O LORD, we beseech thee, let us not perish for this man's life, and lay not upon us innocent blood: for thou, O LORD, hast done as it pleased thee. So they took up Jonah, and cast him forth into the sea: and the sea ceased from her raging. Then the men feared the LORD exceedingly, and offered a sacrifice unto the LORD, and made vows. Now the LORD had prepared a great fish to swallow up Jonah. And Jonah was in the belly of the fish three days and three nights.' -KJV

I don't want you to miss this monumental moment. After throwing Jonah off the boat God caused the storm to cease and the men feared God and started making sacrifices and vows. Why is this important? Because, in the beginning of the text none of the other men believed in the God that Jonah served. Which means even through your rebellion you can still win souls. If that ain't enough to shout right there. But I digress.

I truly believe the reason Jonah was able to sleep during that storm so peacefully, because he had already made up in his mind that if this was going to be the end of him. He was okay with it as long as he didn't have to go and deliver the message. But what he didn't know is God already had made provision for him to have a first class transport service ready to get him to his destiny in the time he was set to have already arrived. Ain't God good.

That means no matter what you are going through right now. No matter how far and how fast you try to run from what God has set out for you to do. It's going to get done whether you willingly go or whether you're forced to go. But it will all get done in the time frame God has set forth for it to be done. Think about Pharaoh and the children of Israel. Remember when he wouldn't let them go and everyone suffered because of it. If you're not familiar with the story I do encourage you to read about it. Basically, Pharaoh kept refusing to give the people up and because of his stubbornness God caused the land to go through a series of plagues. I think one of the worst ones yet, was when all of the first born in the land died. It was a very sad time.

One of the take a ways I would love for you to keep in mind, is that it's more rewarding when you just say 'yes'. I know it's easily said than done, but you can really save yourself a lot of trauma by being obedient. There are lessons to be learned with every test and within every trial. And if you've missed the lesson, believe you will go through the test again, and sometimes with different people. But, in reality. How much time do you think you really have on this earth. How many chances do you think the Lord is giving out nowadays. People are dropping left and right. When that day comes, don't you want to be able to say you've done everything asked of you. I know I do. I know I want to hear 'well done, my good and faithful child'. Wouldn't that be grand.

Worship

<u>Terms:</u>

- Worship- the feeling or expression of reverence and adoration for a deity. Show reverence and adoration for (a deity): honor with religious rites.
- Vulnerable- (of a person) in need of special care, support, or protection because of age, disability, or risk of abuse or neglect.
- Available- able to be used or obtained; at someone's disposal.
- Pentecost- The Christian festival celebrating the descent of the Holy Spirit on the disciples of Jesus after his Ascension, held on the seventh Sunday after Easter. The Jewish festival of Shavuoth.
- Holy Spirit- (in Christianity) the third person of the Trinity; God as

spiritually active in the world.

{Webster}

What comes to mind when you hear the word 'worship'. Do you imagine a sanctuary full of people dancing and singing or do you see that same crowd of people lifting their hands and crying out to the Lord in tears. What does worship mean to you? Do you consider yourself a worshiper? Have you ever worshipped before? Yes, I am and I have. Worship for me is when I come to myself and I think about how good God has been to me and I do whatever action that feels right in that moment. Sometimes I may lift my hands and wave them with my eyes closed. Sometimes I find myself crying with a deep passion of gratitude with my eyes closed. Sometimes I may burst out in a song that really speaks to what I'm feeling in that moment and other times I find myself completely silent gazing off into the sky. I don't know if you've ever been in a state where words weren't enough to express your gratitude or even if you've been in a position where the way you're feeling the word doesn't even exist. If you haven't experienced any of what I'm speaking about. I pray that you begin to open yourself up and allow the Lord to come in and find a resting place not in your mind alone, but in your heart. I wish thing for all.

One way you can reach this place is to listen to something that takes you back down memory lane. There is a song I would like to recommend for you to take a listen at is 'Still Here' by this old gospel group of men. It's three older black men in the group. I don't want to name the group because I haven't got permission to place their name here and I don't want any legal issues to arise. But you guys can figure it out with that much of a description. I trust the Lord will guide you. Okay, this is what you do. When you find the song, you want to find you a place either in your house or in your car where you can be alone. You have to be alone to really get this worship thing started. At least to get you to the place of gratitude I need for you to experience. I say this because it takes away the chance of becoming shy or scared to truly open up when you have an audience around.

Now that you're alone, play the song. Relax, and really listen to the words. If nothing happens in the mist of you listening to the words of that song, then baby you need to go and ask someone to pray for you that you know is really trying to live this life and start this process over again. Why I'm certain something is going to happen the first time around, because of your curiosity. Your curiosity is what's going to get you to that place of total surrender, because you're now anticipating for God to show up and sit with you. And, because you've willingly opened the door for Him to come in. He will. I'm so excited for you. This journey and the relationship you're about to build is going to be so rewarding and so fulfilling. I can't help but smile as I think about it for you. I would love to hear about your journey.

Acts 2:1-3

'And when the day of Pentecost was fully come, they were all with one accord in one place. And suddenly there came a sound from heaven as of a rushing mighty wind, and it filled all the house where they were sitting. And there appeared unto them cloven tongues like as of fire, and it sat upon each of them.' -KJV

What's happening in this text? To my understanding in the prior chapter all of the disciples were in the upper room praying asking God for guidance of who should be chosen to take Judas place in the ministry and apostleship. In the mist of their praying the Holy Spirit fell on everyone that was in the room and they started speaking a new language that was unfamiliar, but everyone understood it. Have you ever witness someone speaking in another language in church and they are in full out worship? What I mean is the person is crying hysterically most times and they are sometimes bent over crying. Other times you may see them standing, waving their hands, crying, and speaking in the foreign language. If not, it is definitely a sight to see. The reason you want to be present when this happens because that means the atmosphere is saturated and God is in the building. This is the prime time if any to get a prayer through and know for certain without a doubt that God is there and He's listening. Don't get excited because this is your chance to ask for whatever you want. You want to get excited because the 'I AM' has entered the room and made His presence known and it is truly an honor to be in the mist. This is your time to love on Him. This is your time to tell Him how good and amazing He is. This is your time to thank Him for everything He's done for you up till that moment and thank Him for everything He's going to do for you in the future. This is your time to lay it on thick. This is your time to woo the only One that can turn your life around. The One who can save your soul. The One who can grant you eternal life. The ONLY One that opinion matters. He has arrived.

<Notables>

John 10:27-28

'My sheep hear my voice, and I know them, and they follow me: And I give unto them eternal life; and they shall never perish, neither shall any man pluck them out of my hand.' -KJV

Revelation 3:20

'Behold, I stand at the door, and knock: if any man hear my voice, and open the door, I will come in to him, and will sup with him, and he with me.' -KJV

I couldn't quote this scripture without pointing something so delicate and significant out about it. Here God is saying if you willingly welcome me in I will commune with you. Referencing the topic we were studying in worship. If you open yourself up and allow God into your heart and allow your mind to think over some things you are grateful for. It will set the atmosphere for a divine visitation.

Hebrews 3:15

'While it is said, To day if ye will hear his voice, harden not your hearts, as in the provocation.' -KJV

2 Corinthians 11:2-3

'For I am jealous over you with godly jealousy: for I have espoused you to one husband, that I may present you as a chaste virgin to Christ. But I fear, lest by any means, as the serpent beguiled Eve through his subtilty, so your minds should be corrupted from the simplicity that is in Christ.' -KJV

Be slow to Anger

Terms:

- Slow- moving or operating, or designed to do so, only at a low speed, not quick or fast.

- Anger- a strong feeling of annoyance, displeasure, or hostility.

- Wait- stay where one is or delay action until a particular time or until something else happens.

- Forgive- stop feeling angry or resentful toward (someone) for an offense, flaw, or mistake.

{Webster}

1 Samuel 28:15-19

'And Samuel said to Saul, Why hast thou disquieted me, to bring me up? And Saul answered, I am so distressed; for the Philistines make war against me, and God is departed from me, and answereth me no more, neither by prophets, nor by dreams: therefore I have called thee, that thou mayest make known unto me what shall I do. Then said Samuel, Wherefore then dost thou ask of me, seeing the LORD is departed from thee, and is become thine enemy? And the LORD had done to him, as he spake by me: for the LORD had rent the kingdom out of thine hand, and given it to thy neighbour, even to David: Because thou obeyedst not the voice of the LORD, nor executedst his fierce wrath upon Amalek, therefore hath the LORD done this thing unto thee this day. Moreover the LORD will also deliver Israel with thee into the hand of the Philistines: and tomorrow shalt thou and thy sons be with me: the LORD also shall deliver the host of Israel into the hand of the Philistines.' -KJV

I know you may be wondering what's going on in this text, so I'm going to bring you up to speed. The children of Israel went to Samuel and demanded that he appoint a king over them to rule. They no longer wanted to be ruled by God, but they wanted someone they could see to rule over them. So Samuel went to the Lord and told Him everything that the people were begging for, so the Lord gave them Saul.

And he said, This will be the manner of the king that shall reign over you: He will take your sons, and appoint them for himself, for his chariots, and to be his horsemen; and some shall run before his chariots. And he will appoint him captains over thousands, and captains over fifties; and will set them to ear his ground, and to reap his harvest, and to make his instruments of war, and instruments of chariots. And he will take your daughters to be confectionaries, and to be cooks, and to be bakers. -KJV 1 Samuel 8:11-13

They no longer wanted to live free basically. It was almost as if they enjoyed being in bondage if you ask me. Even though they were freed from it, mentally they were not. So the Lord gave them what they wanted. After some time passed there was a battle in Gilgal where Saul had made an offering unto the Lord that he was not supposed to make which caused the Lord to be angry with him because of his disobedience. When Samuel had arrived and saw what Saul had done. He then told him that God was angry with him and He was going to raise up another king to take Saul's place. Shortly after that, there was another battle against Amalek. And the Lord wanted Saul to destroy every thing and every one due to Him wanting to avenge his people. But, when Saul got over there he didn't do what God had instructed him to do. He ended up sparing the king Agag and taking all of the goods that were in good condition as a gift to himself. And that angered God even more to a point to where He no longer dealt with Saul.

Now, the Philistines gathered their armies for battle to go up against Saul's army and they brought their champion Goliath. No one was able to defeat Goliath and it put fear in Saul. But, there came one. David a young whipper snapper and he was willing to defeat Goliath in hopes of freeing his father's house in Israel. After he defeated Goliath, Saul wanted him to stay in the palace. After about a few winnings in war. The women started singing praises over David comparing him to Saul in favor of David, and that didn't sit to well with Saul. He became jealous and sought to kill David.

Saul hunted David, and David continued to run. The cat and mouse chase went on and on until one day David had the upper hand on Saul but he chose to spare his life. You would think that would make Saul no longer want to chase after him, but it didn't. Which leads us to where we are in text. The Philistines had rose up against Saul again and David was amongst them. Out of fear for his life, Saul sought to speak with the Lord about the coming battle and the Lord wouldn't answer him. Out of desperation Saul went to a woman with a familiar spirit for her to summon Samuel from the dead to see if he can get a word from the Lord.

When Samuel came he questioned why did he summon him and let him know everything that the Lord had warned him of in the beginning of his first betrayal/disobedience was about to come to pass. Death was going to be his portion and it was nothing he could do about it.

1 Samuel 31:1-6

'Now THE Philistines fought against Israel: and the men of Israel fled from before the Philistines, and fell down slain in mount Gilboa. And the Philistines followed hard upon Saul and upon his sons; and the Philistines slew Jonathan, and Abinadab, and Melchishua, Saul's sons. And the battle went sore against Saul, and the archers hit him; and he was sore wounded of the archers. Then said Saul unto his armourbearer, Draw thy sword, and thrust me through therewith; lest these uncircumcised come and thrust me through, and abuse me. But his armourbearer would not; for he was sore afraid. Therefore Saul took a sword, and fell upon it. And when his armourbearer saw that Saul was dead, he fell likewise upon his sword, and died with him. So Saul died, and his three sons, and his armourbearer, and all his men, that same day together.' -KJV

The is ultimately what happens when you go against what God instructs you to do. As you can see it started out with one rebellion that escalated into many. I believe if Saul would've learned from his first mistake maybe then the Lord would've spared him. But, then again once God say something pertaining you believe it's going to happen. One of the things I wanted us to focus on was the rage Saul had against David which was kindled from jealousy. He spent the bulk of his last days trying to kill someone that had nothing against him.

What are some things that trigger that feeling of rage in you? Do you get angry fast? If so, that's something you can start adding into your daily prayers that the Lord helps you control. I know this is a area I tend to struggle with myself. I think the biggest issue for me which causes me to become angry steams from my impatience. Even while driving, if someone cuts me off on the streets or if there is a traffic backup. I tend to feel rage over something I can't control. Because I am aware of these issues that I still have personally. Believe I will start pointing these things out as well to ask God to remove it from me. This journey is not easy. And if anyone tells you they don't get angry they are lying. The only advise I can give in these type situations that I've learned from my studies of the word is: when in anger sin not. Which means yes you will get angry, but don't do anything that will cause you to sin. Try to walk away instead of retaliating. Easier said than done, but let's try and make the effort.

<Notables>

James 1:19-20

'Wherefore, my beloved brethren, let every man be swift to hear, slow to speak, slow to wrath: For the wrath of man worketh not the righteousness of God.' -KJV

Proverb 16:32-33

'He that is slow to anger is better than the mighty; and he that ruleth his spirit than he that taketh a city. The lot is cast into the lap; but the whole disposing thereof is of the LORD.' -KJV

Matthew 6:14-15

'For if ye forgive men their trespasses, your heavenly Father will also forgive you: But if ye forgive not men their trespasses, neither will your Father forgive your trespasses.' -KJV

Matthew 18:21-22

'Then came Peter to him, and said, Lord, how oft shall my brother sin against me, and I forgive him? till seven times? And Jesus saith unto him, I say not unto thee, Until seven

*times: but, Until seventy times seven.' -*KJV

This means no matter how many times someone does something to hurt you, you have to forgive them and move forward. Now that doesn't mean not to use the wisdom that God gave you pertaining to dealing with that person. If you know someone keep doing things to hurt you and you keep forgiving them, you don't have to stay around them to keep giving them chances to do something else. Be smart.

Patience

Terms:

- Patience- the capacity to accept or tolerate delay, trouble, or suffering without getting angry or upset.
- Antsy- agitated, impatient, or restless.
- Reflect- think deeply or carefully about.
- Relief- a feeling of reassurance and relaxation following release from anxiety or distress.
- Depressed- in a state of general unhappiness or despondency.

{Webster}

Job 2:1-7

'AGAIN THERE was a day when the sons of God came to present themselves before the LORD, and Satan came also among them to present himself before the LORD. And the LORD said unto Satan, From whence comest thou? And Satan answered the LORD, and said, From going to and fro in the earth, and from walking up and down in it. And the LORD said unto Satan, Hast thou considered my servant Job, that there is none like him in the earth, a perfect and an upright man, one that feareth God, and

eschewweth evil? and still he holdest fast his integrity, although thou movedst me against him, to destroy him without cause. And Satan answered the LORD, and said, Skin for skin, yea, all that a man hath will he give for his life. But put forth thine hand now, and touch his bone and his flesh, and he will curse thee to thy face. And the LORD said unto Satan, Behold, he is in thine hand; but save his life. So went Satan forth from the presence of the LORD, and smote Job with sore boils from the sole of his foot unto his crown.' -KJV

How did we get here. Job was a favored man by God. He did everything he was supposed to do and he loved God with all of his heart and God loved him. He had everything you could ask for during that time and an abundance of it. Well one day the Lord called a meeting and in that meeting he bragged on Job to Satan of how upright he was and how he chose good over evil. And Satan goes and say that Job feared God without cause because God protects him greatly. So, to put Satan's theory to the test and to prove him wrong the Lord allowed him a chance to go after Job.

When Satan took everything from Job and came to the realization that Job still wasn't going to turn against God, he became more frustrated and angry. So when the LORD called everyone to him again and he asked Satan what he had been doing. Satan was like, going back and forth in the earth. And God was like, so what happened with Job. And Satan basically was like, he's still committed to you but if you allow me to afflict his body. I know he would turn on your for sure. And then God was like, ok, give it your best shot. But he knew and trusted that Job was true unto him.

During the test of loosing his family and his flocks and becoming ill. There was a point later on in the text where you began to notice that Job got depressed. But, he still never cursed God.

MY SOUL is weary of my life; I will leave my complaint upon myself; I will speak in the bitterness of my soul. I will say unto God, Do not condemn me; show me wherefore thou contendest with me.' -KJV Job 10:1-2

Have you ever felt as though your situation was unbearable? Have you ever been in a low state in your life where you couldn't tell up from down or your right from left. Figuratively speaking of course. What did you do in that situation or should I ask what do you do in those situations. Can you honestly say you pray your way through and wait on God to come and recue you? Or, do you take matters into your own hands? There is a blessing in waiting and allowing the Lord to fight your battles for you.

I encourage you to finish reading the story of Job. What you will find is that he never cursed God. Now, he may have cursed the day he was born. But, he never said anything to condemn himself regarding the LORD. Through his patience and strength to endure, Job was blessed with more than what he'd lost. What have you gained since your last obstacle that made up for the struggle you went through? God still has more that He wants to bless you with, but are you willing to hang in there when the tides becomes to high to ride.

Patience is hard. I am a witness to the struggle of enduring when you feel like giving up. I can also bare witness to the times when I get angry because I want whatever the thing I'm hoping for to happen when I want it to happen and it don't. Patience is definitely another request that we all should keep in our prayer requests. The more we work at the more we will grow as believers and dowers of the word. This battle is not ours alone and believe me when I say, you are not the only one struggling. You'd be surprised at how many people struggle with patience. I just think we are the only ones willing to admit it. Smile, because we are closer to mastering it than we were yesterday.

<Notables>

James 1:4

'But let patience have her perfect work, that ye may be perfect and entire, wanting nothing.' -KJV

Hebrews 6:11-12

'And we desire that every one of you do show the same diligence to the full assurance of hope unto the end: That ye be not slothful, but followers of them who through faith and patience inherit the promises.' -KJV

Rest

Terms:

- Rest- cease work or movement in order to relax, refresh oneself, or recover strength. {An instance or period of relaxing or ceasing to engage in strenuous or stressful activity.}
- Relax- make or become less tense or anxious.
- Refresh- give new strength or energy to; reinvigorate.
- Restore- return (someone or something) to a former condition, place, or position.

{Webster}

How often do you take time for yourself? I mean really. I consider myself one of the hardest working lazy person ever created. I take pride in pampering my lazy. I know it don't sound right, but it's my truth. I don't mind working two jobs. I'll sign up for overtime. I'll even volunteer for a twelve hour shift as long as I can afford to be lazy after. I enjoy taking naps in the middle of the day. I enjoy getting my nails done and going to the movies. I've recently became a member of a spa near my home all for the sake of relaxation. There is nothing like having a moment to gather yourself and recharge. You only have one you and if you don't properly take care of yourself. You can shorten your life span all from exhaustion. Let's see what the good book has to say about it.

Genesis 2:1-3

'THUS THE heavens and the earth were finished, and all the host of them. And on the seventh day God ended his work which he had made; and he rested on the seventh day from all his work which he had made. And God blessed the seventh day, and sanctified it: because that in it he had rested from all his work which God created and made.' - KJV

It took God six days to form the world and everything in it. One thing that I noticed in reading is that he rested at night and only worked during the day. How many of us work during the evenings? I remember when I was a security officer. I used to work the overnight shift sometimes to make some extra money. Now when I think about it. Every job that I've had I've worked the evenings and have worked on the weekends as well. There was a point in my life when I worked two jobs for eight years straight. Don't ask me how I did it, just know that I did. I think I was on some get money type thing. (Laughs out loud)

When you look at what God has done in six days there is no comparison to anything we've ever tried to do ourselves. If he can do that and take a break then why can't we take a break. What is it that makes us feel like if we don't do something that day and finish, it'll never get done. Or, if we don't signup for those extra hours. We'd never have enough money to cover whatever it is we are needing or wanting to pay. Just that sentence alone has opened up an area in my brain that has never been opened before. Here I am sitting at my desk working a twelve hour shift today, yesterday, and tomorrow as if God isn't going to make a way for me as he always have. Like he ain't going to breathe on my situation as he has done in the past. Oh what little faith I have. That's an eye opener. Are you facing the same circumstance and I. Or, have you ever been in this predicament before? Lets make an effort to add this into our daily prayers as well. Ask that the Lord give us the courage to trust that he will continue to provide for us and meet our needs as we make an effort to rest more. Can you say 'anxiety attack', knowing that you are mentally making a conscious decision to act on what you say you're going to allow God to do. You're asking God to teach you how to be a REAL dependent. That is huge! That is major! That is a big deal! I don't care what no one says, that is a BIG DEAL.

I'm stressing the nature of the task because at some point in our lives we have trained our minds to be independent. Everything that we do, we have this thought process of 'I did this' and no one else. Sometimes we can even attest to the fact that we haven't given credit where credit is due. All the credit belongs to God, because the fact of the matter is if he didn't allow you to open your eyes. Nothing of what you've done so far could've ever manifested. Once that fact sunk in. I've made a conscious effort to always give the glory and the honor to the one who truly deserves it and that's to God. Now, I do still need help in that other area which is rest. (Laughs hysterically). However, I do know in time and with enough prayer. It will come.

Make time for God. I wanted to be sure I shed some light on this point before we moved on to our next topic. Don't think of that day of rest for just rest. Think of it as a time to commune with God. What have you done for or said to God lately. Are you one of those people that only speaks to him or acknowledge him when you are in need. Have you ever had one of those friends or family members that you only hear from when they need to borrow twenty dollars or spend the night over your house for a few days until they can go back home. And, you never hear from them again until something else comes up. Don't be that person. Especially not with God. He is the ONLY one that has been there with you and he is the only one that has never left you. He is the ONLY constant in your life that has and will never change. No matter how bad things get or have gotten. He has always and will always be there. You owe it to him to give him some of your time. Remember he gave it and he can take it away.

<Notables>

Exodus 30:8-10

'Remember the sabbath day, to keep it holy. Six days shalt thou labour, and do all thy work: But the seventh day is the sabbath of the LORD thy God: in it thou shalt not do any work, thou, nor thy son, nor thy daughter, thy manservant, nor thy maidservant, nor thy cattle, nor thy stranger that is within thy gates:' -KJV

Whatever day you consider your sabbath, you shouldn't lift not one finger. Not even to clean the house. I know there has been confusion going on in our times of whether Saturday or Sunday is the true sabbath and to be honest I really don't know. I was raised to go to church on Sundays and to not work on Sundays. However, as I grew and came into the knowledge myself. I've learned that Saturday may actually be the Sabbath.

In conclusion, my plan is this. I'm going to still go to church on Sundays due to that's when my church host their services. But, I'm going to be lazy on Saturdays just incase that is the day I am not supposed to lift a finger. I don't know which day you set aside to follow this command. But, for me and mine. We are going to try and reverence both days. But, Sunday

I still plan on cooking and cleaning on that day because I'm usually at my most tiredness on Saturdays. Go to God in prayer for how you should handle your reverence day.

Mark 6:31-32

'And he said unto them, Come ye yourselves apart into a desert place, and rest a while: for there were many coming and going, and they had no leisure so much as to eat. And they departed into a desert place by ship privately.' -KJV

Here, we see these people went into a private space to rest. Do you have a place set aside in your home for God? Because I live alone, I talk to God all over the house. (Laughs out loud). I know it might sound strange, but I do. My favorite place in my home to speak with him is when I'm downstairs relaxing on the couch. This is the best place in the house to me because there's a huge window that sites behind the sofa and you can just lay down and look directly in the sky. It makes me feel as though I'm talking directly to him. And when I'm there and in that relaxed state, we have that opportunity to crack a whole lot of jokes.

I recognize things are going change when I get married and children comes into play. Because that means I will no longer have that freedom and will have to find another more intimate space to commune with my God. But I trust He will provide another space for us to chat it up. Last but not least, my second favorite place to speak with God is in my car. Oh, the conversations and the prayers we have in that thing. I know whoever go my old car is a blessed individual. The tears and the work that went on in that automobile is impeccable if I do say so myself. I enjoy riding down the expressway listening to a nice reverent gospel song to get me in the place I need to be to welcome God into the passenger seat for a chat. Man ol' man. You talk about a sight to see. It gets deep.

Psalm 127:2

'It is vain for you to rise up early, to sit up late, to eat the bread of sorrows: for do he giveth his beloved sleep.' -KJV

Now this right here is enough to shout off of. Do you realize how much weight I could've not gained if I went to bed earlier than I already do. And, how much sleep I can actually have if I woke up later than 6 a.m.. Just let this verse marinate.

Exodus 23:13

'Six days thou shalt do thy work, and on the seventh day thou shalt rest: that thine ox and thine ass may rest, and the son of thy handmaid, and stranger, may be refreshed.' - KJV

RIGHTEOUS

What does righteousness means to you? Have you ever thought about it? Is there really a standard way of doing things to be considered righteous. I don't have all of the answers, but I'm sure there is a standard in the bible for us to follow. I am certain we can use Jesus as an example of how we should carry ourselves and his walk would be the perfect example we should all want to replicate. I believe we all have a desire to want to live righteously and it's evident because of our efforts to continue to educate ourselves in the word.

Forgiveness

Terms:

- Forgive- stop feeling angry or resentful toward (someone) for an offense, flaw, or mistake.
- Mercy- compassion or forgiveness shown toward someone when it is within ones power to punish or harm.
- Renew- resume (an activity) after an interruption.
- Compassion- sympathetic pity and concern for the sufferings or

misfortune of others.

- Grudge- a persistent feeling or ill will or resentment resulting from a past insult or injury.

- Obeisance- a gesture expressing deferential respect, such as a bow or curtsy.

{Webster}

Genesis 37:1-4

'And Jacob dwelt in the land wherein his father was a stranger, in the land of Canaan. Theses are the generations of Jacob. Joseph, being seventeen years old, was feeding the flock with his brethren; and the lad was with the sons of Bilhah, and with the sons of Zilpah, his father's wives: and Joseph brought unto his father their evil report. Now Israel loved Joseph more than all his children, because he was the son of his old age: and he made him a coat of many colours. And when his brethren saw that their father loved him more than all his brethren, they hated him, and could not speak peaceably unto him.' -KJV

Within the first few verses we can already sense a spark of jealousy going on between the children, because the father which was Israel has chosen a favorite. I haven't had the pleasure of birthing children of my own yet, but I hope I don't chose a favorite. I know first hand what it feels like to feel as though someone else is favored over you. The preferential treatment is real. I can relate to what these fellas were feeling and I can relate to Joseph also, because I have been the favorite before as well. Let's continue and see what happens now that Joseph has been gifted something none of the other children were given.

5-11

'And Joseph dreamed a dream, and he told it his brethren: and they hated him yet the more. And he said unto them, Hear, I pray you, this dream which I have dreamed: For,

behold, we were binding sheaves in the field, and, lo, my sheaf arose, and also stood upright; and, behold, your sheaves stood round about, and made obeisance to my sheaf. And his brethren said to him, Shalt thou indeed reign over us? or shalt thou indeed have dominion over us? And they hated him yet the more for his dreams, and for his words. And he dreamed yet another dream, and told it his brethren, and said, Behold, I have dreamed a dream more; and, behold, the sun and the moon and the eleven stars made obeisance to me. And he told it to his father, and to his brethren: and his father rebuked him, and said unto him, What is this dream that thou hast dreamed? Shall I and thy mother and thy brethren indeed come to bow down ourselves to thee to the earth? And his brethren envied him; but his father observed the saying.' -KJV

Okay, these verses informs us in a nutshell that Joseph is a dreamer and the dreams he's been having lately are predicting his future. In this future he is going to be ruling over his family in some way and they are going to bow or be servant unto him and his brothers aren't taking this prediction too well. At this point, none of them know what the dreams mean. However, it gives the other siblings more reason to hate Joseph. Don't miss how Israel started thinking about what Joseph said.

12-19

'And his brethren went to feed their father's flock in Shechem. And Israel said unto Joseph, Do not thy brethren feed the flock in Shechem? come, and I will send thee unto them. And he said to him, Here am I. And he said to him, Go, I pray thee, see whether it be well with thy brethren, and well with the flocks; and bring me word again. So he sent him out of the vale of Hebron, and he came to Shechem. And a certain man found him, and, behold, he was wandering in the field: and the man asked him, saying, What seekest thou? And he said, I seek my brethren: tell me, I pray thee, where they feed their flocks. And the man said, They are departed hence; for I heard them say, Let us go to Dothan. And Joseph went after his brethren, and found them in Dothan. And when

*they saw him afar off, even before he came near unto them, they conspired against him to slay him. And they said one to another, Behold, this dreamer cometh.' -*KJV

Have you ever had someone plan to do you harm? Or have you ever planned on doing harm to someone else? I remember this one time back when I was in middle school. There were some kids in my neighborhood that me and my brother us to play with and I would always get into a physical fight with them. One night me and the other girl was having one of our usual disputes and while I sat on the sidewalk and she stood a few steps away. I was plotting how I was going to attack her, because I had gotten fed up with hearing her mouth. I had this glass bottle in my hand from a drink I had just finished and I broke it and charged at her. Some of the guys standing around caught me and made us fight fair. However, after they got the glass out of my hand. I went in for the first punch.

How would you feel if it was a family member trying to bring harm to you though. I can't imagine no matter how angry my siblings may make me. I can't imagine ever wanting to bring harm to them outside of a punch to the face. Anything outside of that is unsettling. I love them all too much to ever want anything bad to happen to them.

20-28

'Come now therefore, and let us slay him, and cast him into some pit, and we will say, Some evil beast hath devoured him: and we shall see what will become of his dreams. And Reuben heard it, and he delivered him out of their hands; and said, Let us not kill him. And Reuben said unto them, Shed no blood, but cast him into this pit that is in the wilderness, and lay no hand upon him; that he might rid him out of their hands, to deliver him to his father again. And it came to pass, when Joseph was come unto his brethren, that they stript Joseph out of his coat, his coat of many colours that was on him; And they took him, and cast him into a pit: and the pit was empty, there was no water

in it. And they sat down to eat bread: and they lifted up their eyes and looked, and, behold, a company of Ishmeelites came from Gilead with their camels bearing spicery and balm and myrrh, going to carry it down to Egypt. And Judah said unto his brethren, What profit is it if we slay our brother, and conceal his blood? Come, and let us sell him to the Ishmeelites, and let not our hand be upon him; for he is our brother and our flesh. And his brethren were content. Then there passed by Midianites merchantmen; and they drew and lifted up Joseph out of the pit, and sold Joseph to the Ishmeelites for twenty pieces of silver: and they brought Joseph into Egypt.' -KJV

I don't know if it's just me or if I'm just overly sensitive, but I felt those words. The part when they said they sold him to the Ishmeelites. I think not only did I feel betrayed. There was an ounce of disbelief, disappointment, and shame as if I was he. How could they do this to their own flesh and blood. Did you feel it?

Genesis 43:15-26

'And the men took that present, and they took double money in their hand and Benjamin; and rose up, and went down to Egypt, and stood before Joseph. And when Joseph saw Benjamin with them, he said to the ruler of his house, Bring these men home, and slay, and make ready; for these men shall dine with me at noon. And the man did as Joseph bade; and the man brought the men into Joseph's house. And the men were afraid, because they were brought into Joseph's house; and they said, Because of the money that was returned in our sacks at the first time are we brought in; that he may seek occasion against us, and fall upon us, and take us for bondmen, and our asses. And they came near to the steward of Joseph's house, and they communed with him at the door of the house, And said, O sir, we came indeed down at the first time to buy food: And it came to pass, when we came to the inn, that we opened our sacks, and, behold, every man's money was in the mouth of his sack, our money in full weight: and we have brought it again in our hand. And other money have we brought down in our hands to buy food: we

cannot tell who put our money in our sacks. And he said, Peace be to you, fear not: your God, and the God of your father, hath given you treasure in your sacks: I had your money. And he brought Simeon out unto them. And the man brought the men into Joseph's house, and gave them water, and they washed their feet; and he gave their asses provender. And they made ready the present Joseph came at noon: for they heard that they should eat bread there. And when Joseph came home, they brought him the present which was in their hand into the house, and bowed themselves to him to the earth.' -KJV

What have you noticed so far? So far, we can see that the dreams that Joseph had when he was younger are now coming to past. His brothers are now bowing unto him for he is in a position of power over them. The uniqueness of this situation is the fact that they don't even know it's him yet for he has concealed his identity. No matter what we do in this life, remember what goes around comes around.

27-30

'And he asked them of their welfare, and said, Is your father well, the old man of whom ye spake? Is he yet alive? And they answered, Thy servant our father is in good health, he is yet alive. And they bowed down their heads, and made obeisance. And he lifted up his eyes, and saw his brother Benjamin, his mother's son, and said, Is this your younger brother, of whom ye spake unto me? And he said, God be gracious unto thee, my son. And Joseph made haste; for his bowels did yearn upon his brother: and he sought where to weep; and he entered into his chamber, and wept there.' -KJV

When I read this story for understanding I cried. Not like a ugly cry, but a pity cry. I felt bad for Joseph. No one should ever have to experience what he went through, especially not from your siblings. To be betrayed, sold into slavery, and endure the pain of being away from your parents without them even knowing what happened to you. Is enough to crack. To make matters even worse be expected to face the people that betrayed you and have the heart to feed them in their time of need. I don't think I could've personally have done this. I know it may be wrong for saying this, but I do like the way he took advantage of the situation by having them fear being in trouble for stealing. I think that was a nice vengeful touch. But to see his hurt. They really hurt him. I even wonder if they ever thought about what has become of him over the years. Did they regret what they'd done. Did they miss him.

31-34

'And he washed his face, and went out, and refrained himself, and said, Set on bread. And they set on for him by himself, and for them by themselves, and for the Egyptians, which did eat with him, by themselves: because the Egyptians might not eat bread with the Hebrews; for that is an abomination unto the Egyptians. And they sat before him, the firstborn according to his birthright, and the youngest according to his youth: and the men marveled one at another. And he took and sent messes unto them from before him: but Benjamin's mess was five times so much as any of their's. And they drank, and were merry with him.' -KJV

Let's look at this from another view. Did you notice anything? Let me share with you what I've just witnessed. I saw a group of brothers dinning together and having a good time with someone they thought was a stranger, but was actually their younger brother in disguise. This is something that has never been done throughout Josephs life. Think about it, when they were kids. They hated Joseph because of the favoritism from their father. And to now be able to feast in peace with the people you love deeply only because they don't know it's you. Man, can you imagine the way he felt. What if this was something he had always yarned for. The acceptance of his brothers. To only get it because they don't know it's you and they are trying to avoid not going to prison or getting sentence to possible death by thievery.

Is there anyone in your life that you've done this to knowingly or unknowingly. I know my relationship with my siblings are estranged for reasons I can't possibly make sense of. I know everyone would have their own stories to tell of why we don't keep in touch. But, for me. My answer is consistent around the board. I'm usually the only one that puts forth an effort to reach out and after awhile it becomes tiresome. In my research I've found if I don't put forth an effort to contact them. I won't hear from them. I've come to no longer allow it to bother me and I use this time to pursue after God. I know in His timing that everything will come full circle. Sometimes He calls us to isolation so He can do a work on and through us for His glory.

Genesis 45:1-8

'Then Joseph could not refrain himself before all them that stood by him; and he cried, Cause every man to go out from me. And there stood no man with him, while Joseph made himself known unto his brethren. And he wept aloud: and the Egyptians and the house of Pharaoh heard. And Joseph said unto his brethren, I am Joseph; doth my father yet live? And his brethren could not answer him; for they were troubled at his presence. And Joseph said unto his brethren, Come near to me, I pray you. And they came near. And he said, I am Joseph your brother, whom ye sold into Egypt. Now therefore be not grieved, nor angry with yourselves, that ye sold me hither: for God did send me before you to preserve life. For these two years hath the famine been in the land: and yet there are five years, in the which there shall neither be earing nor harvest.' -KJV

God prepared Joseph for this assignment. He revealed unto him through his dreams what his position would be as an adolescent. He wasn't specific of when it was going to happen or how. He just gave him a glimpse of what was to come. I believe if the Lord would've showed Joseph in detail how he would obtain his position he might've tried to go against the plan. If he knew that his brothers were going to sell him before hand in order for Gods plan to be manifested. I think they would've tried to come up with a plan to delay the process or try to avoid it all together. If someone told you that you would be stripped from your family for the survival of many others. I don't think any of us would be willing to make the sacrifice because our attachment is to great. We would try to make sense of why it have to be us and no one else. Who would voluntarily put themselves through that emotional turmoil and all of the other issues joseph had to endure while on his journey.

When you look at what came out of Joseph's tribulation, aren't you glade that he made it through the test. Many people were fed when nothing could be produced. We are here today because of his obedience because we are all a part of this bloodline. Generations and generations were able to spring forth over a temporary emotional trauma. If you continue to read on you'd find that Joseph was reunited with his father and he still was able to make amends with his brethren. It makes me think back on some of the trials I had to overcome in order for God to get the glory and even get me to this place where I can share some of these testimonies from the bible and even my own testimonies with you. What God has for you is for you and if He said you are going to have something or be something. You can bet your bottom dollar on the fact that it will come to past. You may not know when, how, or in what way it's going to come to into fruition. You can be still and know that Gods word is yes and amen and it NEVER fails.

<Notables>

Ephesians 4:31-32

'Let all bitterness, and wrath, and anger, and clamour, and evil speaking, be put away from you, with all malice. And be ye kind one to another, tenderhearted, forgiving one another, even as God for Christ's sake hath forgiven you.' -KJV

Matthew 18:21-22

'Then came Peter to him, and said, Lord, how oft shall my brother sin against me, and I forgive him? till seven times? Jesus saith unto him, I say not unto thee, Until seven times: but, Until seventy times seven.' -KJV

2 Corinthians 2:5-8

'But if any have caused grief, he hath not grieved me, but in part: that I may not overcharge you all. Sufficient to such a man is this punishment, which was inflicted of many. So that contrariwise ye ought rather to forgive him, and comfort him, lest perhaps such a one should be swallowed up with overmuch sorrow. Wherefore I beseech you that ye would confirm your love toward him.' -KJV

Luke 6:37

'Judge not, and ye shall not be judged: condemn not, and ye shall not be condemned: forgive, and ye shall be forgiven:' -KJV

Repent

Terms:

- Repent- feel or express sincere regret or remorse about one's wrongdoing or sin.
- Regret- feel sad, repentant, or disappointed over (something that has happened or been done, especially a loss or missed opportunity).
- Humility- a modest or low view of ones own importance;

humbleness.

- Burden- a load, especially a heavy one.

{Webster}

Acts 3:1-7

'Now Peter and John went up together into the temple at the hour of prayer, being the ninth hour. And a certain man lame from his mother's womb was carried, whom they laid daily at the gate of the temple which is called Beautiful, to ask alms of them that entered into the temple; who seeing Peter and John about to go into the temple asked an alms. And Peter, fastening his eyes upon him with John, said, look on us. And he gave heed unto them, expecting to receive something of them. The Peter said, Silver and gold have I none; but such as I have give thee: In the name of Jesus Christ of Nazareth rise up and walk. And he took him by the right hand, and lifted him up: and immediately his feet and ankle bones received strength.' -KJV

Okay, there's a man that sits at the gate everyday panhandling. His issue is he can't walk. It wasn't something that happened overtime, he was born this way. So one day when Peter and John was going to pray he asked them for some money but told him they didn't have none but can give him something much more valuable. Which was offering him Jesus. The man accepted the offer and immediately his body was healed.

8-16

'And he leaping up stood, and walked, and entered with them into the temple, walking, and leaping, and praising God: And they knew that is was he which sat for alms at the Beautiful gate of the temple: and they were filled with wonder and amazement at that which had happened unto him. And as the lame man which was healed held Peter and John, all the people ran together unto them in the porch that is called Solomon's, greatly wondering. And when Peter saw it, he answered unto the people, Ye men of Israel, why

marvel ye at this? or why look ye so earnestly on us, as though by our own power or holiness we had made this man to walk? The God of Abraham, and Isaac, and of Jacob, the God of our fathers, hath glorified his Son Jesus; whom ye delivered up, and denied him in the presence of Pilate, when he was determined to let him go. But ye denied the Holy One and the Just, and desired a murderer to be granted unto you; And killed the Prince of life, whom God hath raised from the dead; whereof we are witnesses. And his name through faith in his name hath made this man strong, whom ye see and know: yea, the faith which is by him hath given him this perfect soundness in the presence of you all.'
-KJV

After the lame man was healed in Jesus name, all of the people were amazed at the sight of him walking. And Peter was like why are yall so shocked and amazed at this mans healing when he had nothing to do with the healing. All it took was for the man to believe in Jesus and have faith that he could be healed through Christ. What are you facing today that you are in need of a right now miracle? How big is your faith? I know everyone profess to have faith but no one ever admits when their faith has been shaken or tested.

I am one to admit I have had plenty of times where I was going through something and I couldn't see my way out and you know how you go and confide in your mom and all she say is pray about it or trust God. Do you know how many times in those moment I didn't want to hear that because in that moment (second) I didn't believe, because I couldn't personally see how it could be done. The only advise I can give you when you are in this type of situation that has helped me push through was throwing my hands up literally in the air and saying 'I give up, Lord you handle it'. And as soon as I truly give it up. He makes a way and my faith is renewed (laughs out loud). You can't continue to live as though your faith is never tested.

17-21

'And now, brethren, I wot that through ignorance ye did it, as did also your rulers. But those things, which God before had shewed by the mouth of all his prophets, that Christ should suffer, he hath so fulfilled. Repent ye therefore, and be converted, that your sins may be blotted out, when the times of refreshing shall come from the presence of the Lord. And he shall send Jesus Christ, which before was preached unto you: Whom the heaven must receive until the times of restitution of all things, which God hath spoken by the mouth of all his holy prophets since the world began.' -KJV

Here, we see Peter is giving the people an opportunity to make things right. He has brought their ignorance to their attention and is giving them a chance now that they have been made known of their wrong doings to repent. Lets look back on some things that we've done ourselves out of ignorance in our past. Have we talked about someone? Have we made mention of someone else's misfortune to another that knew nothing about the situation in the name of gossip. Have we took change from our parents that was lying around the house or in the car without them knowing that we took it? I know in your mind you may have justified the act by saying it's just change or maybe you didn't think twice about it because to you it was just change. However, the fact still remains that you were stealing. I've done that several times as an adolescent to my mom and my grandma when I would see change laying around, but at some point I realized what I was doing and I stopped. I haven't repented for the act until just now as I'm typing this sentence. But look at how long it's been since the act was done but I never thought to ask God for forgiveness.

It's very easy for us to slip into sin. Majority of the time we don't even think about it, it's almost as if the act is second nature. However, if we strive to make an effort to be more conscious of what we are doing then maybe we can remember to repent more often. We will never be perfect and if any one says something different it's a lie. All we can do is give our best try and in that I truly believe God blesses and acknowledges our try. What is it that you want to get off your chest and lay at the Lords foot. Now is the time. You don't have to wait for an audience, your audience is already watching, waiting, and listening. Don't be afraid, open your mouth and repent. God loves you, I love you, and everything is going to be alright. Smile.

<Notables>

2 Chronicles 7:14

'If my people, which are called by my name, shall humble themselves, and pray, and seek my face, and turn from their wicked ways; then will I hear from Heaven, and will forgive their sin, and will heal their land.' -KJV

Luke 13:3

'I tell you, Nay: but, except ye repent, ye shall all likewise perish.' -KJV

Proverbs 28:13

'He that covereth his sins shall not prosper: but whoso confesseth and forsaketh them shall have mercy.' -KJV

Matthew 4:17

'From that time Jesus began to preach, and to say, Repent: for the kingdom of heaven is at hand.' -KJV

Distractions

Terms:

- Distractions- a thing that prevents someone from giving full attention to something else. Extreme agitation of the mind or emotions.
- Agitation- a state of anxiety or nervous excitement.
- Frustration- the feeling of being upset or annoyed, especially because of inability to change or achieve something.
- Annoy- irritate (someone), make (someone) a little angry.
- Procrastination- the action of delaying or postponing something.

{Webster}

Matthew 26:40-45

*'And he cometh unto the disciples, and findeth them asleep, and saith unto Peter, What, could ye not watch with me one hour? Watch and pray, that ye enter not into temptation: the spirit indeed is willing, but the flesh is weak. **He went away again the second time, and prayed, saying,** O my Father, if this cup may not pass away from me, except I drink it, thy will be done. **And he came and found them asleep again: for their eyes were heavy. And he left them, and went away again, and prayed the third time, saying the same words. Then cometh he to his disciples, and saith unto them,** Sleep on now, and take your rest: behold, the hour is at hand, and the Son of man is betrayed into the hands of sinners.*

Jesus went to seek God's face in prayer to get guidance of what it was he was supposed to do. He was praying asking if it was truly God's will for him to die for the people and if it was so, his will be done. Before he went up to pray he asked his disciples to keep watch while he went up to do so. Being that he knew there were people after him, it was important that he had someone alert to warn him if someone came. After praying for a while, Jesus came down to check on his disciples and he found them sleeping. It bothered him that he asked them to do one thing and they failed that task by allowing sleep to befall them. We can argue the premise of them falling asleep and saying if the shoe was on the other foot and it was you, you would've stayed woke. But what has distracted you in your life from something you were supposed to complete and you've allowed something so simple as sleeping to keep you away from it.

I love using myself as an example to keep myself on the alter and to show that all of us fall short in more areas then most. Take me completing this book as an example. I started working on this work in 2018 back in August I believe. And you know what, I didn't pick it up again until this July 2019. I can't blame my reasons for not finishing on other things except pure laziness. Even now today being Saturday, September 28, 2019 I could've easily finished this book in the being of this month but I allowed my desire for sleep to distract me. Not only did sleep manage to get the upper hand, but the thought of having to remain focus conquered my willingness to finish as well. Name something that you haven't finished and the reasons why. Do you plan on making an effort to complete the task now that it has been brought to your attention or have you given up on it all together.

What if the disciples never fell asleep and they were alert when the mob came. Do you think things would've been different. Who's waiting on you to deliver a message or depending on you to bring them that twenty dollars you owe them. What's standing in your way of letting go of procrastination. Is procrastination a hinderance to your growth? It is for me in some cases and it is definitely something I'm going to start adding into my prayers for myself. We are all a work in progress. However, it's up to you to decide if you're willing and ready to make the efforts to start filling in and closing those gaps.

<Notables>

1 Peter 5:8

'Be sober, be vigilant; because your adversary the devil, as a roaring lion, walketh about, seeking whom he may devour.' -KJV

1 Corinthians 10:13

'There hath no temptation taken you but such as is common to man: but GOD is faithful, who will not suffer you to be tempted above that ye are able; but will the temptation also make a way to escape, that ye may be able to bear it.' -KJV

Mark 4:19

'And the cares of this world, and the deceitfulness of riches, and the lusts of other things entering in, choke the word, and it becometh unfruitful.' -KJV

The Conspiracy

<u>**Terms:**</u>

- Conspire- make secret plans jointly to commit an unlawful or harmful act.
- Resist- withstand the action or effect of.
- Greed- intense and selfish desire for something; especially wealth, power, or food.
- Entitled- believing oneself to be inherently deserving of privileges or special treatment.

{Webster}

2 Samuel 11:24-27

'And the shooters shot from off the wall upon thy servants; and some of the king's servants be dead, and thy servant Uriah the Hittite is dead also. Then David said unto the messenger, Thus shalt thou say unto Joab, Let not this thing displease thee, for the sword devoureth one as well as another: make thy battle more strong against the city, and overthrow it: and encourage thou him. And when the wife of Uriah heard that Uriah her husband was dead, she mourned for her husband. And when the morning was past, David sent and fetched her to his house, and she became his wife, and bare him a son. But the thing that David had done displeased the LORD.' -KJV

Why is the LORD mad with David, let me explain. There was a war going on in the land and majority of David's men were fighting on behalf of his kingdom. One day David came outside and he saw a woman by the name of Bathsheba out taking a bath and he called for her to come to his palace. When she got there he slept with her and she got pregnant, but the twist is she's married. When David found out that she was with child he sent for her husband to come back to try and trick him into sleeping with her so that they could pass the child off as his. But, when the husband kept refusing to go see his wife. David decided to conspire to have him killed instead. Once Uriah was dead, David then took Bathsheba as his wife.

It's crazy how you can read this story and not get all of the details in the first few sittings, but then when you come back and read it for understanding, you then get all the juice. This is a very interesting story. So interesting that this type of trickery is still going on today. When I finally realized what was going on in this story. I had to read it again to make sure I was reading it right. Have you ever took something from someone and then conspired to fool them out of finding out the truth or convince them that they are the one who'd done the deed? I'm quit confident that none of us have conspired to kill anyone, but , have you conspired in any other way?

What do you make of this story. It's said what's done in the dark will come to the light and the first act was the fact of Bathsheba conceiving. And for David to think he would get away with murder is beyond me. We may can fool man, but there is no fooling God.

12:1-4

'And the LORD sent Nathan unto David. And he came unto him, and said unto him, There were two men in one city; the one rich, and the other poor. The rich man had exceeding many flocks and herbs: But the poor man had nothing, save one little ewe lamb, which he brought and nourished up: and it grew up together with him, and with his children; it did eat of his own meat, and drank of his own cup, and lay in his bosom, and was unto him as a daughter. And there came a traveller unto the rich man, and he spared to take of his own flock and of his own herd, to dress for the wayfaring man that was come unto him; but took the poor man's lamb, and dressed it for the man that was come to him.' -KJV

Does this parable sound familiar to you? Does the example sound like something that just happened?

5-12

'And David's anger was greatly kindled against the man; and he said to Nathan, As the LORD liveth, the man that hath done this thing shall surely die: And he shall restore the lamb fourfold, because he did this thing, and because he had no pity. And Nathan said to David, Thou art the man. Thus saith the LORD GOD of Israel, I anointed thee king over Israel, and I delivered thee out of the hand of Saul; And I gave thee thy master's house, and thy master's wives into thy bosom., and gave thee the house of Israel and of Judah; and if that had been too little, I would moreover have given unto thee such and such things. Wherefore has thou despised the commandment of the LORD, to do evil in his sight? thou hast killed Uriah the Hittite with the sword, and hast taken *his wife to be thy wife, and hast slain him with the sword of the children of Ammon. Now therefore the sword shall never depart from thine house; because thou hast despised me, and hast taken the wife of Uriah the Hittite to be thy wife. Thus saith the LORD, Behold, I will raise up evil against thee out of thine own house, and I will take thy wives before thine eyes, and give them unto thy neighbour, and he shall lie with thy wives in the sight of this sun. For thou didst it secretly: but I will do this thing before Israel, and before the sun.'* -KJV

What a way to have the light shinned on what you thought was covered up. Man, ol man. I never want to be in a position to make God mad with me like this. When Nathan started telling David everything that was about to happen to him. I got scared. This is what it looks like when God passes judgement on you for your actions. Aren't you glad for grace now. Don't get it twisted though, God still punishes us for doing wrong. When you think you've gotten away, you really haven't. I'm just glad that He hasn't judged us to this extreme in this day and time.

<Notable>

Matthew 4:1-4

'Then was Jesus led up of the Spirit into the wilderness to be tempted of the devil. And when he had fasted forty days and forty nights, he was afterward an hungred. And when the tempter came to him, he said, If thou be the Son of God, command that these stones be made bread. But he answered and said, It is written, Man shall not live by bread alone, but by every word that proceedeth out of the mouth of God.' -KJV

When you make the decision to set time aside to commune with God, be assured that the devil will come and try to tempt you. Even if you aren't fasting but have made a conscious decision to try and live right. The tempter will come. Take a look at the first temptation that Satan tried to tempt Jesus with. The one thing that makes all of us weak, food. Have you even been on a fast and it looks like every where you went food was there. Somedays it get so bad people start offering it to you free and you start wondering where were they when you could eat or didn't have the money to purchase something to eat. Don't forget about the free cakes. The problem that I have is every time I decide to go on a fast. My team at my job decides to have a party or my supervisor surprises us with cake or donuts. I'm partaking in a leadership fast today with my church for the entire month of October and we've been given free chicken biscuits this morning. But I'm saving it for later (laughs out loud). Food may feed the body, but the spirit of God feeds the soul.

5-7

Then the devil taketh him up into the holy city, and setteth him on a pinnacle of the temple, And saith unto him, If thou be the Son of God, cast thyself down: for it is written, He shall give his angles charge concerning thee: and in their hands they shall bear thee up, lest at any time thou dash thy foot against a stone. Jesus said unto him, It is written again, Thou shalt not tempt the Lord thy God.' -KJV

Look at this, you see how slick the devil tried to be. He tried to basically tempt Jesus with suicide if you really think about it. Not saying that the Angels wouldn't have come down and helped or even if Jesus couldn't have floated, but it's the fact that he tried to con him into doing something to prove a point. Have you ever had someone bet you that you wouldn't do something so you could prove that you were bold enough to do it. But Jesus corrected him and reminded him of the word that you shouldn't tempt the Lord.

8-11

'Again, the devil taketh him up into an exceeding high mountain, and sheweth him all the kingdoms of the world, and the glory of them; And saith unto him, All these things will I give thee, if thou wilt fall down and worship me. Then saith Jesus unto him, Get thee hence, Satan: for it is written, Thou shalt worship the Lord thy God, and him only shalt thou serve. Then the devil leaveth him, and, behold, angels came and ministered unto him.' -KJV

I just want to take this opportunity to encourage you to stay in the faith. No matter what obstacle may come or who may rise up against you. Remain loyal and under the covering of God. People are going to come into your life and try to sway you. No one ever said temptation wasn't going to come, but the word encourages us to resist. If you refuse to partake in any temptation that comes your way, trust and believe that it will pass. Any good deed done in secret, God will reward you openly. You deciding not to sleep with a married man or woman and turning down their advances is not going or will not go unnoticed. God will reward you in more ways than you can imagine. You deciding not to curse someone out or retaliate against someone that has rose up against you will be rewarded. God will fight that battle for you and when he does don't make light of the situation. Just thank God.

God loves you more than the word 'love' can ever express the depth of his feelings for you. The love between a parent and their child doesn't even begin to scratch the surface of how God feels about us. He is jealous of you. Did you know that. That means there is nothing he wont do or give to you if you only do the things that he ask. We make it harder than what it actually is. We all have work to do, even me. I struggle, but we will get there. Hold on. Help is on the way. You will pass this test.

SEPARATION

Look at how much you've grown. I've purposely referenced 'grown' instead of 'learned', because I believe you've made efforts to correct some behaviors since reading chapter one. We've laughed, we've cried, and we've reminisced on some of our own personal encounters that relate to each topic that was reviewed. And, we can all agree that this journey has been a pleasurable one. Don't stop here. I encourage you to keep learning and to keep growing in the knowledge of the Lord with His guidance. Allow Him to be more involved in helping you make decisions by asking his opinion. Be a friend, not just a dependent. Show Him that you do love him unconditionally and that you want to work on building your relationship the more. There is no greater love and no greater friendship than the one that you have with God. His opinion is the ONLY opinion that matters. Give him space in your life. Make more time to sit and chat with him and allow him to speak to you. Pray, fast, tithe, and be a resource where you can by sharing the word of God to everyone you encounter. Be that light and shine. Impower those that look to you for answers or even those who vent to you. Let the Lord have his way. Be the vessel. Let's finish strong.

The Great Divide

<u>Terms:</u>

- Divide- separate or be separated into parts. (verb) A wide divergence between two groups, typically producing tension or hostility. (noun)
- Separate- cause to move or be apart.
- Isolate- cause (a person or place) to be or remain alone or apart from others.
- Listen- give one's attention to a sound.

{Webster}

Numbers 16:20-26

'And the LORD spake unto Moses and unto Aaron, saying, Separate yourselves from among this congregation, that I may consume them in a moment. And they fell upon their faces, and said, O God, the God of the spirits of all flesh, shall one man sin, and wilt thou be wroth with all the congregation? And the LORD spake unto Moses, saying, Speak unto the congregation, saying, Get you up from about the tabernacle of Korah, Dathan, and Abiram. And Moses rose up and went unto Dathan and Abiram; and the elders of Israel followed him. And he spake unto the congregation, saying, Depart, I pray you, from the tents of these wicked men, and touch nothing of their's, lest ye be consumed in all their sins.' -KJV

Lets do some catching up. After the Lord delivered the children of Israel out of Egypt they were living in the wilderness. Out of frustration I believe is the root of what caused this action a few of the men rose up against Moses and Aaron complaining that they were taken from a place where they had food to a place where they didn't know where there next meal was coming from. When Moses heard all of the accusations that the people were making against them, even saying that he brought them out there so he can be ruler over them. He went to the Lord to seek assistance. After talking with God about all that was going on he went to Korah and told him that the Lord was going to show them who's with him and who's against him on the next day.

When we get down to verse twenty. We start to see the Lord giving instructions to Moses and Aaron of what they needed to do moving forward concerning warning the people. He first told them to separate from the people so he can deal with them and spare Moses and Aaron, but Moses cried out for the people to ask God to allow them an opportunity to choose sides.

27-37

'So they gat up from the tabernacle of Korah, Dathan, and Abiram, on every side: and Dathan and Abiram came out, and stood in the door of their tents, and their wives, and their sons, and their little children. And Moses said, Hereby ye shall know that the LORD hath sent me to do all these works; for I have not done them of mine own mind. If these men die the common death of all men, or if they be visited after the visitation of all men; then the LORD hath not sent me. But if the LORD make a new thing, and the earth open her mouth, and swallow them up, with all that appertain unto them, and they go down quick into the pit; then ye shall understand that these men have provoked the LORD. And it came to pass, as he had made an end of speaking all these words, that the ground clave asunder that was under them: And the earth opened her mouth, and swallowed them up, and their houses, and all the men that appertained unto Korah, and all their goods. They, and all that appertained to them, went down alive into the pit, and the earth closed upon them: and they perished from among the congregation. And all Israel that were round about them fled at the cry of them: for they said, Lest the earth swallow us up also. And there came out a fire from the LORD, and consumed the two hundred and fifty men that offered incense. And the LORD spake unto Moses, saying, Speak unto Eleazar the son of Aaron the priest, that he take up the censers out of the

burning, and scatter thou the fire yonder; for they are hallowed.' -KJV

A lot of people perished because of their ignorance and their unbelief. Most of them didn't know that they had offended God, however, due to their willingness to follow the crowd and what they thought looked and sounded good. They were all put to death within seconds. How many of us can admit to being a victim to someone else's crime. When we were growing up and my mom was passing out whippings to one of my cousins for doing something wrong. Nine times out of ten, she whipped all of us. Even the ones that were guilty by association.

Think of all of the fads that have come and gone throughout your life that may not have been pleasing in the eye sight of God, but you still partook in them. Were you offered an opportunity to choose the righteous way out or was there no other way than to partake. How about today? Are you still doing something knowingly that's not right but making the conscious decision to keep on doing it? What is God was to come back right now and ended the world. What would you do? How would you explain yourself to him? Especially if you get caught red handed. I'm not asking these questions to make you feel bad or anything. I'm asking these questions in hopes to encourage you to start thinking before we react.

I have a lot of work to do myself. I have some habits that only me and God know about and I work daily to try and do better and correct the behavior. Your best try is all that you can give and if you and I keep trying to do better. In time, we'd master no longer falling victim to that offense. Is there someone in your circle right now that you know you need to take some time away from them, but because of loyalty you stay? Loyalty can be the thing that blocks your growth and your blessings. Sometimes God purposely remove people out of our lives to get us to a place where he can do what he needs to do with and through us. It hurts, but it's necessary. I can personally attest to when you've become dependent on someone always being around and you always run to them for any and everything. That be the one that He removes out of your life to get you to depend on him.

I'm grateful for the love that God has for me. When I think back on all of the friendships and or relationships that God separated me from. I'm thankful that he did. I use to hang with some good people, but they were no longer good to or for me. Outgrowing someone is real, but realizing you've outgrown them is a hard pill to swallow. I say this because we have a tendency to dwell on the past, reminiscing on all the things you've overcome together, or all the times you've belled one another out of tough jams. But at what point do you willingly say, 'our time has come to an end'. Aren't you glad for divine intervention. Let's take this opportunity to not only thank God for keeping us and protecting us when we didn't know we needed protection. And, also repent for not choosing his way when we knew right from wrong. I'm so proud of you. Let's keep growing.

Let this mind
"A mind is a terrible thing to waste" – Arthur Fletcher

<u>Terms:</u>

- Mind- the clement of a person that enables them to be aware of the world and their experiences, to think, and to feel; the faculty of consciousness and thought. A persons intellect.

James 1:1-8

James, a servant of God and of the Lord Jesus Christ, to the twelve tribes which are scattered abroad, greeting. My brethren, count it all joy when ye fall into divers temptations; Knowing this, that the trying of your faith worketh patience. But let patience have her perfect work, that ye may be perfect and entire, wanting nothing. If any of you *lack wisdom, let him ask of God, that giveth to all men liberally, and upbraideth not; and it shall be given him. But let him ask in faith, nothing wavering. For he that wavereth is like a wave of the sea driven with the wind and tossed. For let not that man think that he shall receive any thing of the Lord. A double minded man is unstable in all his ways.' -*KJV

I know it can be hard making decisions sometimes. I struggle myself. I wanted to shed light on this topic briefly just to say in all things, seek the Lord. If you ever find yourself in a place of confusion. Seek God. If you lack wisdom. Seek God. If you don't know which way to turn. Seek God. If you have trouble with staying focus, open your bible. In all things, seek God.

<Notables>

Philippians 2:5
*'Let this mind be in you, which was also in Christ Jesus.' -*KJV

Proverbs 23:7
*'For as he thinketh in his heart, so is he: Eat and drink, saith he to thee; but his heart is not with thee.' -*KJV

The Sower

<u>**Terms:**</u>
- Sower- someone who sows to scatter (seed) over land, earth, etc, for growth; plant. To implant, introduce, or promulgate; seek to propagate or extend; disseminate:
- Harvest- the process or period of gathering in crops.

- Selfless- concerned more with the needs and wishes of others than with one's own; unselfish.

- Reap- receive (a reward or benefit) as a consequence of one's own or other people's actions.

- Mission- an important assignment carried out for political, religious, or commercial purposes, typically involving travel.

- Purpose- the reason for which something is done or created or for which something exists.

1 Kings 17:8-11

'And the word of the LORD came unto him, saying, Arise, get thee to Zarephath, which belongeth to Zidon, and dwell there: behold, I have commanded a widow woman there to sustain thee. So he arose and went to Zarephath. And when he came to the gate of the city, behold, the widow woman was there gathering of sticks: and he called to her, and said, Fetch me, I pray thee, a little water in a vessel, that I may drink. And as she was going to fetch it, he called to her, and said, Bring me, I pray thee, a morsel of bread in thine hand.' -KJV

I encourage you to take some time to read the book of Kings to get familiar with what took place during this time to get a full understanding of the story of Elijah. After Elijah called for the heavens to be shut up and produce no rain. The Lord told him to go eastward to hide and he would provide food and water for him to live off of. When the brook of Cherith went dry the Lord then sent Elijah to Zarephath to dwell and had prepared a place for him to stay. When God sends you somewhere, trust he will provide for your every need.

12

'And she said, As the LORD thy God liveth, I have not a cake, but an handful of

meal in a barrel, and a little oil in a curse: and, behold, I am gathering two sticks, that I may go in and dress it for me and my son, that we may eat it, and die.' -KJV

Here, we see where Elijah had asked the lady for something to eat after he arrived and this is where she explained she didn't have a whole lot to share.

13-16

'And Elijah said unto her, Fear not; go and do as thou hast said: but make me thereof a little cake first, and bring it unto me, and after make for thee and for thy son. For thus saith the LORD God of Israel, The barrel of meal shall not waste, neither shall the curse of oil fail, until the day that the LORD sendeth rain upon the earth. And she went and did according to the saying of Elijah: and she, and he, and her house, did eat many days. And the barrel of meal wasted not, neither did the curse of oil fail, according to the word of the LORD, which he spake by Elijah.' -KJV

Has someone ever asked for your last? If so, were you willing or unwilling to give it? A widow woman was asked by a prophet to give him her last first and then she'd have enough for herself and her son after. Lets think about if this was us. I know if I were her and Elijah said this to me I wouldn't have believed him because I couldn't see how his words could be so. I hear what you are saying but I know and I see what's in my barrel. For this lady to do as she was told and ask no questions after. I need that type of faith. That type of faith is like the faith the woman with the issue of blood had. The type of faith that moved Jesus to bless the woman who he compared to a dog. The type of faith Abraham had when he took Isaac up to offer as a sacrifice all because he trusted God's will and he plan for his life. That type of faith right there. I need that, I desire that.

17-24

'And it came to pass after these things, that the son of the woman, the mistress of the house, fell sick; and his sickness was so sore, that there was no breath left in him. And she said unto Elijah, What have I to do with thee, O thou man of God? art thou come unto me to call my sin to remembrance, and to slay my son? And he said unto her, Give me thy son. And he took him out of her bosom, and carried him up into a loft, where he abode, and laid him upon his own bed. And he cried unto the LORD, and said, O LORD my God, hast thou also brought evil upon the widow with whom I sojourn, by slaying her son? And he stretched himself upon the child three times, and cried unto the LORD, and said, O LORD my God, I pray thee, let this child's soul come into him again. And the LORD heard the voice of Elijah; and the soul of the child came into him again, and he revived. And Elijah took the child, and brought him down out of the chamber into the house, and delivered him unto his mother: and Elijah said, See, thy son liveth. And the woman said to Elijah, Now by this I know that thou art a man of God, and that the word of the LORD in thy mouth is truth.' -KJV

One thing I want to point out and shed light on. Is the fact that God will never ask you to do something for him and then not do something for you in return. As I pondered on this story, who's to say that this woman's son wasn't already pre-destined to die and God sent Elijah to her not only to sustain him, but to bless her and pray for her son. Has that thought ever crossed your mind. She may not have had the right in the beginning to go to God and ask him to heal her son, but because of her sacrifice it opened a window for her to make a request of him. Ain't that deep. Don't get me wrong, I'm not saying that's the case. I'm just saying look at every situation from another aspect.

Think about if she would've turned Elijah away and not blessed him. Then, when the sickness overtake her son. Who and of what authority would she have to request of God to help her save her son. God could've easily at that time could've been like 'what about when I asked you to see about my profit I sent that you turned away'. However, because of her obedience and her willingness to do as the man of God asked of her. She was able to ask for assistance when she needed it the most.

What have you done for the Lord lately? Is there something that the Lord has asked you to do and you haven't done it yet. If it is, don't feel bad because if you are reading this sentence that means He has given you an opportunity to do what it is he is required of you to do. We really don't recognize how merciful the Lord is towards us. We are a blessed people and it's time to start giving thanks and honor where honor is due. No man on this earth can do what they are doing without the permission from God. He allows a certain amount of freedom to give us an opportunity to make the right choice, which of course is to choose him. However, there is a timer on his leniency. Trust me. When that day comes where your expiration has come on this earth. I pray that we all have made the right decision and have chosen God as our one and only love and Jesus as our savior. Go in peace. You can do this.

ABOUT THE AUTHOR

From the author that brought you 'The Ultimate Betrayal, The Next door Neighbor, Hazel Eyes, and Watch This'. Danielle Walker has delivered another ground breaking novel. Danielle is an Atlanta native with a passion for Christ and a great love for I Am (God). She serves on the leadership board at A Work in Christ Ministries where she serves besides her mom Pastor Carmela Cole and her dad Bishop LeRoyal Monte Cole. Her gift of writing has been a blessing to her and she wanted to use it to honor her God by writing and dedicating this novel to him. In hopes of it reaching the unlearned, the unsaved, the backslidden, the saved, and the newly professed believers to assist with their journey of becoming whole. She believes there is only one true and living God and the only way to him is through Christ. And no matter where she is or what she's writing, she wants to let it be known that she loves and adores her God and would love to offer him to everyone her path crosses. This book was written at her ripped age of thirty.